MODELLING AND SCULPTURE

DETAIL OF SCULPTURED RELIEFS BY LUCA DELLA ROBBIA FROM THE *CANTORIA*, OR MUSICIANS' GALLERY, NOW IN THE MUSEUM OF S. MARIA DEL FIORE, FLORENCE.

MODELLING AND SCULPTURE

A PRACTICAL TREATISE FOR STUDENTS, WITH A BRIEF HISTORY OF THE ART

By

F. J. GLASS

Headmaster of the School of Arts and Crafts, Doncaster
Author of "Drawing, Design, and Craftwork"
"Sketching from Nature," Etc.

NEW YORK
CHARLES SCRIBNER'S SONS
LONDON: B. T. BATSFORD LTD.
1929

First Published 1929

MADE AND PRINTED IN GREAT BRITAIN BY
THE ABERDEEN UNIVERSITY PRESS LTD., ABERDEEN
FOR THE PUBLISHERS
B. T. BATSFORD LTD., LONDON

PREFACE

THIS book, the outcome of twenty years' teaching experience, has been written with a desire to help students who are struggling to express themselves in plastic materials, and those who wish to appreciate modelling and sculpture without desiring actually to practise the art. The methods advocated are based upon the great works of the past, and a careful study of nature's handiwork. There are many opportunities for the student proficient in plastic art, and monumental sculpture and statuary are not the only means by which the modeller or carver can earn a livelihood. Skilled men are needed for wood and stone carving, for terra-cotta and pottery of all kinds, for the production of models for bronze casting and other forms of metalcraft, and generally for the interior and exterior decoration of buildings. There is a great tradition in sculpture as in painting, literature, and music; and there are wonderful works in each branch of art which we cannot possibly ignore if we would acquire a comprehensive and correct knowledge of the thoughts and aspirations of yesterday and to-day—for to-day is the inevitable outcome of the days which have preceded it. There is much to learn from the past, and it is only by learning it thoroughly that we can hope to add our quota to the progress of this and future ages. In this spirit of humility and gratitude to the giants of bygone days the present book is offered to students, whether they are actually working in plastic materials or wishing to appreciate the art of modelling and sculpture.

I am indebted to Mr. Douglas Sayce for many of the photographs which illustrate the various lessons, to Mr. Francis Shurrock and Mrs. G. F. Watts for allowing me to include the examples on Plates XII. and XV., and the top illustration on Plate XLV. respectively, to my publishers, Messrs. Batsford, and to Mr. Harry Batsford in particular, for their generous assistance, and to Mr. E. Fuller Fabian and the late Professor E. Lanteri who helped me first to appreciate and work in plastic materials. Of the Historic Sculpture plates, Plate XXXIII. is reproduced from a photograph by Mr. F. H. Crossley, F.S.A., of Chester, whilst a number of others are from subjects in the British Museum, Victoria and Albert Museum, and from photographs in the publishers' collection.

F. J. G.

DONCASTER, *April*, 1929.

v

CONTENTS

CHAPTER I.

SIMPLE MODELLING.

Value of Modelling.—The moulding of forms in the round in some plastic material, such as clay, plasticine, or wax, has many advantages over drawing, or the graphic representation of form in one plane only. Modelling necessitates a realisation and a grasp of the form, so that it may be rendered from every point of view, deeper and more complete than drawing, where one view only is attempted. Hence a closer and more analytical study is needed for modelling, and the student is well advised to take a course in this subject, even though sculpture is not his speciality, for the knowledge of form thus acquired is of inestimable value in all the arts, whether plastic or graphic. The portrait painter, who thoroughly understands the bony framework, the sections, and underlying forms of the head, knowledge which can only be obtained by actually moulding these forms in the round, will be better able to suggest the solidity and "relief" of his subject than another painter who has worked in one plane only. The same remarks apply to the figure, and in fact to all branches of art where form plays any part. Time spent in modelling is time well spent, whatever may be the ultimate aim of the student, besides which there is a satisfaction in actually making a form, in realising its solidity and multiplicity of contours, that a representation on one plane only, of one contour only, can hardly be expected to give.

Materials and Elementary Forms.—The first consideration for the student is the nature of the material. He must acquire familiarity with the medium so that he may express himself freely and easily, for clay presents considerable difficulties to the beginner, especially if he is ambitious and essays too much at the outset. We will therefore begin at the very beginning, assuming that the student is starting young, as we hope will be the case generally before long; even as in drawing the attention is now first directed to the earliest scribblings of the child. The natural start then is with those forms most easily obtained in clay, plasticine, or modelling wax. Of these the best and most easily handled is clay, but in the elementary school where the classes are large and the teacher's time well occupied, plasticine or other similar medium is preferable, being more easily kept in condition and less liable to make a mess. Each pupil should be provided with a slate, or preferably a small board about 14 ins. by 10 ins., a lump of plasticine or modelling paste and a simple boxwood tool. Almost any sort of tool is suitable for the first lessons; a match stick serves very well. Children love making things and generally enjoy these lessons if intelligently taught, and it is hardly necessary to say that more is achieved when the interest is aroused than when the lesson is dull and dreary, whilst the knowledge of

I

form so acquired is undoubtedly of great educational value. The forms most easily obtained in the plastic material are balls and egg shapes, which can be rolled between the hands. These can be made to resemble fruits, loaves of bread, footballs, pine-cones, acorns, and even simple animal and bird forms, by combining, and by incising dots and strokes with the end of the match or tool. Interest is created in this way and the value of the lesson much enhanced. A glance at Plate I. (a) will show a few of the possibilities along these lines. The next stage will be a flattening of these forms by pressing with the finger and thumb, after which they may be combined and shaped to resemble flowers, leaves, bean pods, etc. Plate I. (a) shows a few of the shapes obtainable in this way. Further developments will occur to the teacher, but the limitation of space makes it impossible to go more fully into the subject here. Following upon a few such lessons as these the pupils might be given a simple leaf form such as the laurel, bay, rhododendron, privet, or lilac to model (Plate I. (b)) after the teacher has pointed out its characteristic features. At first its shape and the depression at the centre where the mid-rib divides the leaf will be found sufficient, but later the undulation of the surface and the value of light and shade in showing this might be pointed out. They should be taught to realise the fact that generally one side of the leaf is in shade whilst the other catches the light (if lit from the side)—this being dependent upon the angle formed by the two sides at the mid-rib. The greater strength of this mid-rib compared with the more delicate veins, and the bosses and concavities that make up the surface of the leaf, will all afford material for the exercise of eye and hand. Leaves of more complicated contour should next be attempted, such as the oak, vine, sycamore, ivy, nasturtium, etc. (Plate I. (b)), and later a spray of leaves. Here the difficulties are multiplied, for to the variety in the leaves is added the arrangement on the twig and the delicate drawing in the joints, where there is often a tiny resting bud set between the leaf stalk and the main stem (Plate I. (c)). The teacher must see that these matters receive proper attention, for there is a tendency to avoid difficult details. If the spray is laid upon a board the relative heights of the various portions above the board can readily be seen, and the student should be instructed to realise that a similar variety in relief must be given to the clay. He should be taught that a mere drawing of leaf shapes is insufficient; that the undulation of surface and edge must also be rendered to give a " live " representation of the plant. Flower forms (Plate I. (d)) also furnish excellent material for the student, who should at first attempt single blossoms, and afterwards the whole plant. Decorative renderings might well be essayed also, taking as suggestions for treatment the Tudor-rose, the Gothic ball-flower, and the four-petal flower used in the Gothic diapers; and many others that occur in the historic examples available. A further addition should be made to the modelling tools at this stage, and a couple of wire tools introduced. Plate II. shows a fairly complete set from which selections can be made. In the elementary school it is rarely possible to go farther than this with modelling, if so far, but this book being intended for the modelling student in particular we will proceed. It is a pity that the work should have to break off so suddenly, as it does under our present system. It would be better if modelling was carried much further and made a necessary part of education through all its stages, for the human race has always expressed its highest aspirations in the plastic as well as the graphic arts and a keener appreciation of modelling would lead to a deeper insight into the thoughts and feelings of those to whom we owe our present civilisation. Besides which a greater knowledge and love of the beautiful is developed, which certainly adds a zest and interest to life, and I am convinced tends to make it more happy and healthy. This unfortunately is either not recognised at all, or lost sight of, by our utilitarian educationists. To return to our subject. The student having thus learned something of his materials, of form, and light and shade in these early lessons will find the later ones easier and more interesting in consequence. It has already been pointed out that modelling depends for its effect upon light and shade, and that light and shade depends upon surfaces, and the position of these surfaces with regard to the light. These surfaces in modelling are generally spoken of as " planes," for however smooth and round a shape may be it can be analysed and broken up into a series of planes. The first thing the student must learn then is how to see these surfaces and to appreciate their relationship one to another and to the light. A modelling that presents the appearance of having had all its rounded surfaces turned up on the lathe will be dull and lifeless when compared with another where the same surfaces are composed of planes or facets upon which the light rests squarely and the half tones and shadows are broad and vigorous. The human figure is made up of these flat surfaces, although the general effect is that of subtly rounded forms. Subtle indeed they are, and only by a due rendering of the planes can this subtlety be approached. The next lesson should be one in which surfaces play the most important part. Plate I. (e) illustrates a few examples of simple forms easily modelled and dependent entirely upon the play of surface. Planes sweeping and twisting so that sometimes they face the light and sometimes are turned from it, broad smooth surfaces and sharp depressions afford excellent practice in designing for relief work, and in acquiring facility in handling clay. I say clay, for it is easily the most sympathetic material, and the student who intends to model seriously should begin at once to familiarise himself with this the best of all mediums for plastic expression.

Tools and Materials.—The tools and materials necessary are : A board for working on ; the size of this will depend to some extent upon the work in hand, but a clamped half Imperial 15 ins. by 22 ins. is a good size (Fig. 4). A sponge for keeping the fingers damp. A few modelling tools and some clay. The latter should be of the right consistency, for if too hard the difficulty in manipulation renders free expression almost impossible, whereas if it is too soft it clings to the hands and clogs the tools. Practice alone will enable you to judge the consistency, but it is better to work a softer clay over a harder. In other words, commence with clay fairly stiff and build up with it, then with softer clay you may spread the forms you require over the harder clay below. This is essential as the stiff clay below offers sufficient resistance and allows of spreading the softer upon it. If you attempt to reverse this proceedure you will find your hard clay embedding itself in the softer clay below, which immediately loses its shape. Remember that modelling is the reverse of carving. Modelling is adding to, carving is taking from. In the former you commence with nothing and build up, while in the latter you commence with too much and cut away. Keep this fact in mind and let every bit of clay you put on be an essential part of the scheme. Do not put on too much clay and then carve it away if you can avoid it. It is a waste of energy and is less vigorous in appearance than work directly applied.

Handling of Clay.—Having supplied yourself with board, sponge, tools, and clay, set your board on an easel or stand a little below eye level and damp the board.   Take a lump of fairly stiff clay and roll it between the hands until it assumes a rough cylindrical form ; this is fairly easy to draw with and can be spread on the damp board.   Rolling the clay between the hands helps to make it even in consistency and more easily worked ; it also helps to remove hard lumps, which are most annoying when they crop up, especially if one is engaged in modelling some delicate form.   Practice spreading the clay with the thumb and fingers, keeping them damp with the sponge, contrast concave surfaces with convex, bosses with depressions, and so learn something of what your medium is capable, and at the same time store the mind with suggestions for design and treatment.   Plate I. (*e*) shows a few examples : many more will occur to you as you progress.   Another useful exercise is to cut some strips of paper, roll them into scrolls, and then translate into clay (Plate I. (*f*)).   The paper will be found to be full of suggestions for treatment.   I say treatment, for it is no use attempting to get the thin edge of the paper, if you did it would not only appear thin and meagre but would crumble away.   But the play of light and shade on the curved surfaces will provide an interesting lesson, very valuable when later you introduce scrolls, cartouches, etc., into your heraldic and other designs.   Plate I. (*f*) gives a few examples developed in this way. These lessons are valuable for acquiring facility in handling the material and also in giving you a feeling for surface.

Historic Study.—The next exercise should be an attempt to copy some good example of historic ornament.   The work of past sculptors is a veritable treasure-house for the student.   Here he will find the solution to many of the problems that will from time to time occur to him.   An intelligent study of historic work is the finest possible training.   The student is advised to keep his sketch book handy and make drawings of any piece of ornament that appeals to him.   It may be only a leaf or a flower, or a piece of abstract ornament, but make a note of it, and by so doing fix it in the memory for future use.   Or if it be a matter of planes and treatment that appeals, model it in clay, and so find out exactly wherein its beauty lies.   The copying of a large piece of ornament, especially if it contains a quantity of work that does not appeal to you, is often a tiresome business, and of doubtful value except as an exercise in determination and patience.   It is better to take some good examples of a certain style and make a design from them.   You may take your motif and treatment from the examples, but arrange them in your own way.   This brings the creative instinct into play and adds much interest to the work, besides being good training in design.   More will be said of historic work in another section.

Preparing Ground for Modelling.—Having chosen a good cast that appeals to you place it on a stand or easel on a level with the background upon which you propose to work.   To prepare the background take some strips of wood 1 in. or 1½ ins. thick and cut them to the size required. Nail these strips to a board so that they enclose a space the size you wish your background to be (Fig. 1).   Damp this space with the sponge, roll the clay up in your hands and press it on the damp board within the strips. When sufficient clay has been applied level the surface flush with the strips, by means of a straight-edge (Fig. 1).   The framework enables you to give a perfectly smooth, level surface to your clay.   With a boxwood tool sketch in the main lines of the ornament, and commence to build up.

PLATE I.

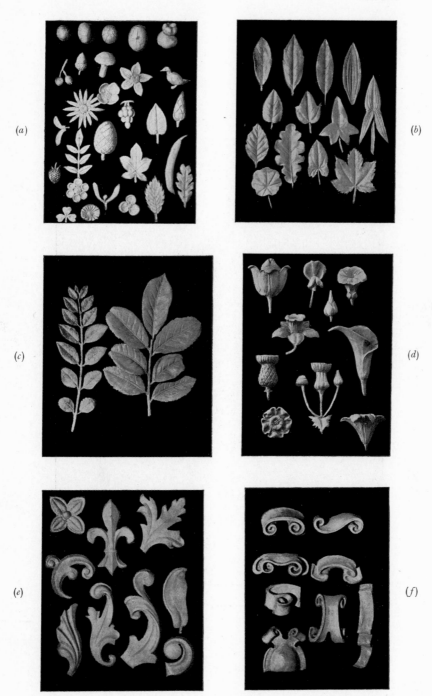

ELEMENTARY MODELLING—SUGGESTIONS FOR BEGINNERS.

PLATE II.

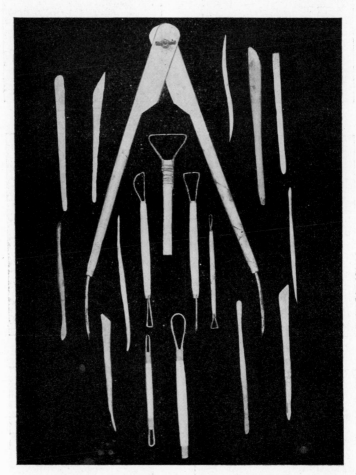

MODELLING TOOLS.

Building-up.—Let the clay used for the ground be stiffer than that used for the modelling, and that used for building-up stiffer than that used for the later stages, reserving the softest for finishing.   Should the work require keeping, it must be covered with a damp cloth to preserve its condition.   When the work is rough it does not matter if you lay the cloth directly upon the clay, but as soon as you begin to put surface modelling into it, the cloth must not be allowed to come into contact with the clay.   To avoid

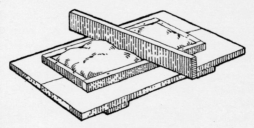

FIG. 1.—Preparing a Background.

this you may either stick a few wooden pegs into the less important parts of the work and allow the cloth to rest upon these, or make a framework of wood to stretch the material across.   A piece of American cloth over the damp cloth will preserve the work in good condition for two or three days.   And it is essential that the clay should be kept in good condition, for it is very disheartening to attempt to work upon clay that is too hard to yield to treatment, or to add other clay to, for the soft clay will not adhere properly to hard stuff from which the moisture has evaporated.   So that time spent in keeping the work in condition is time saved in modelling.

Copying.—In copying the ornament before you, watch carefully for the directions of planes or surfaces; note the relative projections of various portions. Aim at the big things first; get the projections and the broad directions of surface before attempting the more delicate planes and surface modelling.   When the work tires you and your enthusiasm flags, it shows that interest has evaporated and it is probably better to throw the work away, but be quite sure that you have got all the good you can out of it, and that laziness is not the reason for your lack of interest.   As before stated, it is better to start a design of your own in some historic style than to copy slavishly some piece of ornament, however good it may be, especially if you have lost your enthusiasm.   You will find it necessary to return again and again to historic examples for suggestions in design and treatment.   It is absurd to think that you can design something absolutely original, without reference to the work that has already been produced. Progressive art must be related to the art that has gone before ; it is a gradual growth, and if you would advance you must be familiar with the best work of the past.   No student of literature would dream of writing until he had learnt his language, the result of ages of evolution in the art of expression.   The art student too must learn his language or he can never hope to express himself intelligently.   It is true that much modern work seems to ignore all that has gone before.   The tendency with the ultra-moderns appears to be towards crude, archaic forms, absolutely devoid of beauty or scholarship.   For them the Greeks and the great artists of the Renaissance, or the earnest workmen of the Gothic seem never to have existed.   To judge by these modern productions art might be in its earliest stages, when it struggles with but little skill and less knowledge to express it knows not what.   But this is merely a passing phase ; there are many such phases in the history of artistic expression, and it will disappear. But unfortunately it is very distracting to the student, who cannot help being influenced by the work that is produced around him. He should remind himself, however, that fashions are always changing, and that many influences are brought to bear upon art, as upon every other mode of expressing thought. He should, therefore, study work that has lived, for the verdict of time is a safer verdict than that pronounced by changing fashion. His standard must be beauty; if he cannot see beauty in a work, he should eschew it. Let him compare these crude, modern productions with the work of Phidias and Michelangelo, and if he prefers the crude, modern to the fine, older work, it will be because he prefers novelty to lasting beauty. Novelty soon palls, even though it may charm for a time; it is better, therefore, to steep the mind in the work that has lived, for your own work will then possess permanent qualities altogether lacking in the novelties that catch the eye of a fickle public one day and are consigned to oblivion the next.

Space Filling.—The student, having acquired some knowledge of historic ornament, and a feeling for "relief," light and shade, and planes, should practise designing in clay. At first it is perhaps better not to handicap himself by worrying about the material into which clay is ultimately translated. It is safer to confine himself to filling the space at his command harmoniously and easily, until such time as he has gained confidence and a fair control of his medium. He should essay the filling of various shapes such as squares, rectangles, circles, triangles, lunettes, etc., remembering that his effect is dependent upon light and shade. The first thing to decide is the distribution of the masses—the shapes and projection of the principal bosses. Remember that variety is more interesting than equality or monotony. There should be a dominant mass, with other masses subordinate to it, or, if the occasion demands, two or three dominant masses, well spaced and pleasant in form. Having decided upon the spacing and arrangement of the principal masses, the connecting lines and minor masses must be arranged. The height or projection of these with regard to the projection of the dominant masses and the arrangement of the planes must next receive consideration. These matters should, of course, be fixed with due regard for the type of ornament you have decided upon, although it is a good exercise to design purely in mass and plane without taking any natural or artificial motif at all. The ornament so produced will be purely abstract, the outcome of your feeling for design and light and shade, and also for the nature of your medium. Where, however, you are using a motif it must be duly considered in your planning. Your masses must be arranged in such a way that it needs no violation of natural growth, or of ornamental fitness, to get your elements into the shapes you have designed for them.

Fig. 2 illustrates the method of procedure in designing a simple panel. Fig. 2 (1, 4, 7, 9) show the arrangement of the dominant masses. In No. 1 the heaviest and most important mass is at the bottom of the panel, two masses of equal value are placed symmetrically at the top, with minor masses spotted between. Fig. 2 (2) shows these masses brought together by connecting lines and more decided shapes in the ornament. Fig. 2 (3) is more definitely modelled, with the planes thought out, which must be carefully done, with due regard for variety in light and shade. Note that the flower and bud forms are placed at or near the top (with the exception of two smaller flowers used to carry the interest down, and fill in the spaces at either side). The placing of floral forms high up in the panel is in accordance with nature's scheme, and generally it is the right place for them in design. This, however, is no hard and fast rule,

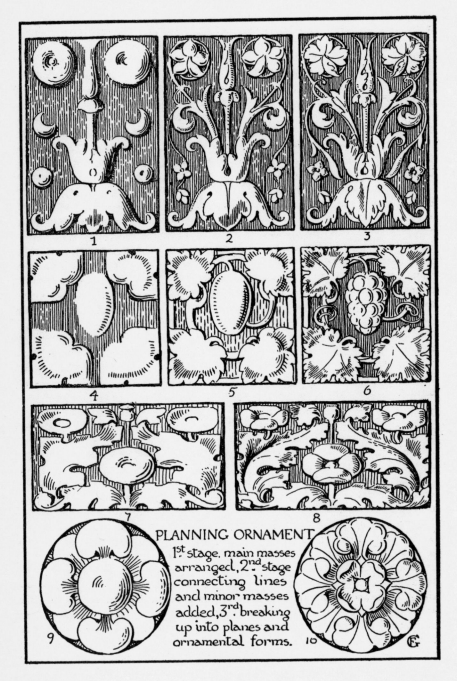

PLANNING ORNAMENT. 1st stage, main masses arranged, 2nd stage connecting lines and minor masses added, 3rd breaking up into planes and ornamental forms.

FIG. 2.

for they may be placed low in the panel quite successfully, but it is a natural law worth remembering. Note, too, that the heaviest mass is at the bottom ; this makes for stability. Fig. 2 (4) is the mass arrangement for a square panel, a mass somewhat above the centre, with four masses grouped about it empha- sising the angles. The two masses at the base are rather larger than the upper ones, and the central mass, though no larger than the others, is yet the most important because of its position and greater interest. It is so placed that the main lines of the composition lead the eye towards it, whilst the other masses encircle it, giving it importance. Its interest is enhanced by the fact that it is composed of fruit, whilst the surrounding forms are leaves. Fig. 2 (5) and (6) illustrate the development of the ornament. Fig. 2 (7) and (8) show the planning of a panel based on the poppy.

In this case the largest flower is rather below the centre, with two smaller flowers placed symmetrically at the top. These three spots which attract the eye by virtue of their interest form a triangle (apex downwards) which is counter- balanced by the opposing lines in the foliage. Here the position of the flower (below the middle) is justified by the shape of the panel and the spreading lines of the growth. Note the square treatment of the leaf edges, which helps to counteract the flowing curves of the design. In the vine panel also the edges of the leaves have been fitted to the square corners. This is in obedience to the rule that corners should always be considered. Rectangles are disting- uished by their corners, they are in fact peculiar to these figures. The corners should, therefore, be emphasised in design. Fig. 2 (9) and (10) illustrate the massing suitable for a rosette. Four equal masses grouped about a larger central one. It is by no means essential that the centre boss should be the largest, but it should certainly be the most interesting owing to its central position. A flower or bunch of fruit surrounded by leaves makes a satisfying rosette. Nature again furnishes us with the prototype for this arrangement. If you take a wood anemone, a rhododendron, or, in fact, almost any growing flower and look down upon it from above (in plan as it were), you will see the central blossom with the leaves grouped about it, radiating from the centre of interest (the flower).

Plant Forms.—When using plants for design it is necessary to conven- tionalise them, to render them suitable for the medium, and also to fit them for purposes of design. Plate III. (a), (c), and (d) are examples of plant study. The exercises previously suggested in the conventional treatment of flowers, leaves, etc., will be of service here. A design should always seem to belong to the space it occupies. If there appears to be the least possibility of taking the design from its position and fitting it into a different one with equally good (or bad) results, it means that the design lacks fitness. There should be some- thing of the inevitable about a design ; the position it occupies and no other is the proper place for it, should be the impression made upon us. No feeling of doubt as to whether it would not be better elsewhere, or whether some other design would not be better in its place, should be permitted to arise. The only way to obtain this sense of fitness, this inevitable quality, is to consider the space to be filled first of all, and to carefully plan the lines and masses in harmony with the space. When these are satisfactorily schemed it is time to turn them into floral, animal, or abstract forms, but not before. A mere copy of a plant, or any other motif, no matter how well it is modelled, placed within bounding lines, will never produce true ornament. It may decorate the space, and appear very pretty to the uninitiated, but to the artist with a feeling for harmony, it can only jar upon his sensibilities. So that, whatever the motif may be, always bear in mind the shape you are filling. Let your lines and masses be well balanced and pleasing, your planes carefully considered, and the details justly subordinated to the general scheme. " The whole is greater than the part," and a well-balanced panel, where each portion of the design is in correct relationship to the other portions, will be far more satisfactory than one in which obtrusive detail (no matter how well modelled) clamours for attention. Don't fritter away the broad light and shade by over empha-sising the detail. It may seem that too much stress has been laid upon this point, but students are so apt to become engrossed with the particular part upon which they happen to be engaged, and to forget the general effect, that it is necessary to reiterate the warning. Consider the work as a whole, plan the masses first, and keep the details subordinate to the main scheme. It is a good plan to view your work from a distance occasionally, so that you may readily grasp the whole, and so keep each portion in proper relationship to to the rest. Plate III. (b) shows a panel based on the early English style.

MODELLING FOR BRONZE, WOOD, STONE, TERRA-COTTA, ETC.

When the student has learnt something of design and the nature of his medium by the exercises in space-filling, he should turn his attention to the materials into which clay is generally translated. Of these bronze, wood, stone, and terra-cotta are perhaps the most important, whilst plaster, leather, and Repoussé metal should not be neglected.

Bronze.—Bronze admits of the utmost freedom in treatment, for any-thing that can be modelled in clay can be cast in bronze. In the section on metal casting the process of casting bronze is described, both by the sand and the waste wax methods. It will be seen from these descriptions how free is the scope in modelling for bronze. A panel intended for re-production in bronze should receive a treatment different from that given to wood or stone. In each case the masses and light and shade must be well considered, but in bronze it is essential that the surface modelling should be varied in texture. The detail may be as fine as you wish, the edges thin and sharp, and the planes may sweep in any direction, there being no grain to worry about as there is in wood. Broken surfaces contrasted with smooth planes look well in bronze. Remember that the high lights will be emphasised by the polish (when smooth) and still further by the dark colour of the metal in the hollows. It is therefore advisable not to have too many large smooth patches but to vary the surface as much as possible so that the high lights may have additional value. If carefully placed these polished surfaces will have a rich jewel-like effect in contrast with the darker, more broken nature of their surroundings. The student should carefully study surface qualities when modelling for bronze, and learn how to make such surfaces rich and interesting. Large plain surfaces are not nearly so valuable in bronze as they are in stone, and herein lies one of the essential differences between the treatments necessary for bronze and stone. When, later on, figure compositions are attempted in the round and in relief the difference between the treatment required for bronze and that for wood and stone will be even more marked. Figures in the round when modelled for bronze may

be much more free in pose and treatment, than figures intended for stone.   A
figure may be poised as if for flight, balanced upon the toes of one foot with
arms outstretched and drapery fluttering, and in bronze would look quite
safe.   In stone such a pose would lead to disaster, for the scanty support afforded
by the one foot in contact with the base would be wholly inadequate for the
weight of stone in the figure.   Fluttering drapery, too, may be much thinner
in bronze, more nearly approaching the delicacy of the actual fabric, than in
stone.   Stone being brittle requires a certain bulk to be strong enough to stand;
bronze is tensile and may, therefore, be wrought into much finer forms.   Stone,
too, should possess an appearance of adequate strength and support, whilst
with bronze we know its tenacity, and so the eye is not offended at a treatment
that would in stone make us shudder.   Study carefully any bronzes (ancient
and modern) with which you may come in contact, and so learn what is suitable for translation into this metal.

   Stone.—The first thing to determine when designing for stone is whether
the material will be a fine close-grained stone or a soft, coarse-grained one.   It
is obvious that the hard, close-grained stone will take a finer finish than the softer
stone.   Marble or alabaster may be finished with the utmost delicacy, which
would be impossible, or lost, in a coarser material.   The next consideration
is the position to be occupied by the carving.   Generally it is placed in an
architectural setting and a due recognition of surrounding mouldings and other
features is of the utmost importance.   Again, its situation with regard to the
eye level needs to be considered.   A design that is to be placed at or near the
eye level may be much more delicate than one that is to be placed far above it.
The lighting, too, is a factor that must be arranged for ; a work that is to occupy
a position where the light is dim will need a stronger treatment than another
that will occupy a well-lighted spot.   It may seem that all these restrictions
are calculated to daunt the student, and to cramp his activities, but a frank
recognition of the limitations and requirements of position and materials
need not daunt or cramp, but rather help by suggesting a suitable mode of
treatment.   Let your ornament be designed in such a way as to form an integral part of the architecture.   It should fit quietly and harmoniously into
the general scheme, an enrichment of the architecture, rather than an obtrusive feature clamouring vulgarly for attention.   When dealing with space-
filling the importance of the bounding lines was insisted upon ; the construc-
tional lines in the building are equivalent to the bounding lines of the panel,
and must be accepted in plotting the ornament.   Emphasise the construction ;
don't attempt to ignore or to disguise it.   Let your ornament appear as though
it grew out of the stone and not as though it were stuck on.   Another thing to
avoid is a relief of such depth that it suggests a hole in the wall.   The architect
arranges his windows and door spaces with due regard for the effect produced
by these openings contrasting with the plain wall space, and he will not thank
you for upsetting his scheme by introducing another dark.   When designing
ornament for a particular position see that your model is exactly the same
size as the stone to be carved, and take care that your relief does not get too
high for the depth of the stone.   It is so easy to keep on adding clay that one
is apt to forget that the stone has a definite limit, beyond which it is impossible
to go.   It is a wise plan to make a rough gauge (Fig. 3) and to run this across
the modelling occasionally to make sure that you keep the projections within
bounds.   Much more might be written on this subject but space is limited.

Figures in stone or marble should be simple in pose and restrained in treatment. The stately poses of the Greek figures and the treatment of the drapery afford excellent examples of what may be attempted in marble. For relief treatment the frieze and metopes of the Parthenon and some of the delicate work of the Renaissance should be earnestly studied.

FIG. 3.—A Gauge.

Wood.—When designing for wood-carving it is well to bear in mind the character of the material, and the tools used. There is a characteristic quality about wood-carving that must be suggested in the clay. Do not forget that in wood as in stone carving you start with more than you require and cut away. Modelling is the exact reverse of this, but when building up a design for carving, add a little more than is necessary, and cut away with the wire or boxwood tools. The design when finished should suggest wood, even as designs for bronze and stone should suggest those materials. It should be possible in each case to tell which material the design is intended for, by the treatment given to it. Gouges and chisels, and a tough fibrous medium in which the grain is an important factor, are the items to be reckoned with. Long sweeping cuts, depressions contrasting with raised portions, convex surfaces with concave, sharp, sparkling edges, with edges that are almost lost in the ground,—these are the characteristics of carving, and these are the qualities to aim at in the design. As with stone, situation must be taken into consideration, and the projections arranged accordingly. Furniture, for example, would require more delicate carving than architectural work, which again would vary according to its position with regard to the spectator. Wood being cut into planks of varied thickness it is necessary to keep the projections within the limits of the wood at our command. As with stone a rough gauge might be used for this purpose (see Fig. 3). It is so easy to keep adding clay, when we feel that a greater projection would improve the effect, that we are apt to exceed the limits of the wood at our disposal. This can only result in disappointment, for you cannot add a bit here and a bit there in wood as you can so easily do in clay, and so it is imperative that the design in clay should be kept within the limitations set by the wood.

Figures carved in wood admit of greater freedom of pose than is the case in stone. The strong fibrous texture is less liable to fracture than the more brittle stone. Hence extended limbs and fluttering drapery will not be so likely to produce a feeling of insecurity in the mind of the observer, when carved in oak, walnut, cedar, etc., as they would in marble. But the obtrusive grain and dark colour of wood is far less pleasing for figure work than is the soft semi-transparent texture of marble. It is more suitable for heavily draped figures of comparatively small size than for nude figures, or figures of large proportions. Again, wood is not advisable for exterior decoration, but rather for interior positions where it is not subjected to the inclemencies of the weather. The small figures so successfully introduced by the Gothic carvers in the internal decoration of their ecclesiastical buildings, afford splendid examples of the right use of wood for this purpose. It is a doubtful material for the representation of the nude figure: knots have a knack of occurring just where they are not required, the grain is likely to be obtrusive, and cracks are apt to appear.   For draped figures, however, especially if the drapery is full and generous in treatment, the texture of wood enhances the quality of the folds. The colour of the material helps to deepen the shadows, while the outstanding folds are brought into greater prominence by the smooth finish that can be obtained in wood.

Terra-cotta.—Terra-cotta being but fired clay, the utmost freedom of handling is permissible.   Practically anything that can be modelled in clay is suitable for terra-cotta.   Here again, however, the ultimate purpose and position of the work must have primary consideration.   The architectural setting must be duly recognised, together with the lighting and the position with regard to the eye level.   Generally a rich, full treatment is preferable, with generous, convex surfaces, contrasted by fairly strong darks.   Textures should also play their part in the scheme ; broken surfaces should be opposed by broad, smooth planes, and the result will be that both are enhanced in value.   When the work is intended for glazing or enamelling, it should be borne in mind that the deepened colour of the glaze, where it collects in the hollows, adds emphasis to the shadows there.   A delicately-patterned surface is of great value in a glazed terra-cotta.   The work of the della Robbias in this branch of art should be earnestly studied.   The wonderful blend of colour and relief in these beautiful productions cannot fail to inspire the student.

PLATE III.

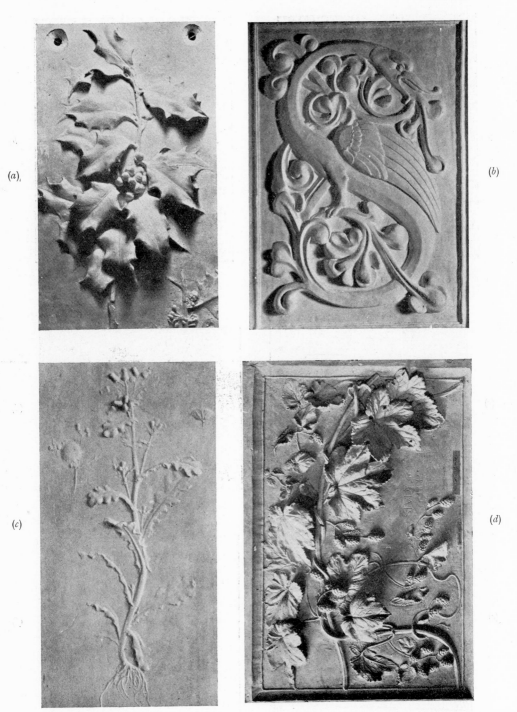

(a) PLANT STUDY. (b) A DESIGN IN THE EARLY ENGLISH STYLE. (c) and (d) PLANT STUDIES.

PLATE IV.

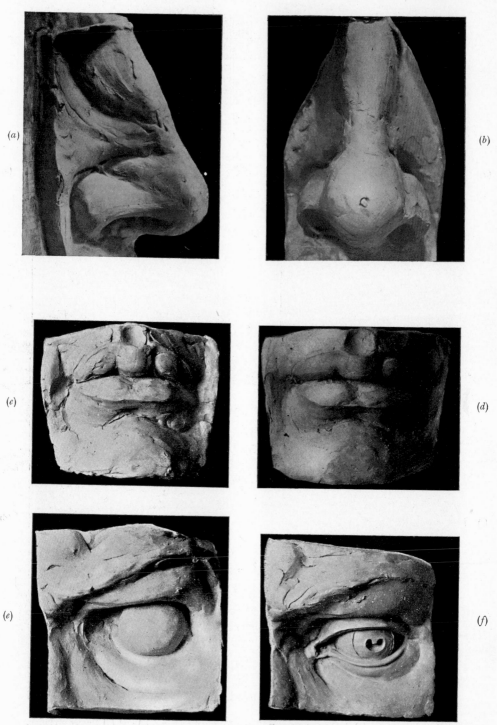

(a)

(b)

(c)

(d)

(e)

(f)

BUILDING UP THE FEATURES.

CHAPTER II.

THE FEATURES.

BEFORE commencing a bust, whether from life or the antique, the student should learn the essential forms of the features by studying each one separately, for then, the difficult task of modelling a head will be simplified by a knowledge of its component parts. The casts of the features from the figure of " David " by Michelangelo are undoubtedly the best examples for purposes of study. They are larger than life size, with a corresponding breadth and vigour of treatment, an emphasising of the essential, and an elimination of the accidental, that makes them invaluable to the student of form.

Basic Form.—There is a certain basic structure underlying all natural forms which is typical and general. In the features under consideration this structure has been seized by the analytical genius of the greatest of the Renaissance sculptors. It is rendered with a truth and precision and an anatomical knowledge that cannot fail to benefit the student who earnestly copies them. For the forms here exhibited underlie all eyes, noses, ears, and mouths, however much they may differ in the individual ; and though often difficult to trace, a knowledge of essential form will teach the student what to look for, and any modification will be at once apparent.

The Nose.—We will commence our study by copying the nose. Provide yourself with a board, a pair of callipers, a sponge, modelling tools, a stand or easel for working upon, a few pegs of wood for fixing measurements, and some clay. The board may be of any convenient size, but should be strong, with a couple of battens screwed to the back to keep the wood from warping when the damp clay is applied (Fig. 4). Fix the board to the easel or stand at about eye-level, and hang the cast of the nose alongside. An easel or stand that can easily be moved is preferable, as it is advisable to work in different lights, for only in this way can the forms be seen and realised. As the mass of clay will be somewhat heavy it is necessary to support the weight by means of a " butterfly." The " butterfly " is composed of two small pieces of wood placed crosswise and bound together with copper wire by means of which it is fastened to a nail driven into the board (Fig. 5). The clay is built around this support, and the subsequent risk of its falling off the board is thereby minimised. Before applying the clay, the board must be sponged over with water, for the clay will not adhere to a dry board. Press well on to the damp surface of the wood a thin coating of clay. Upon this the cast may be placed and the outline traced with a modelling tool. This will give some definite points from which to start your measurements, and will considerably facilitate the work. Now roll the clay between the hands until somewhat cylindrical forms are obtained, and with these gradually build up until the correct projection has been arrived at. Press the clay well together, so that no air spaces may be left, or the work will fall to pieces. The advantage of rolling the clay between the hands lies in the fact that it makes the clay more homogeneous and even in texture, at the same time giving you a definite shape which is easier to model into the correct form, than

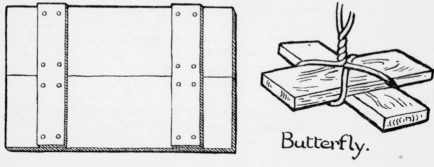

Butterfly.

FIG. 4.—Modelling Board.   FIG. 5.

would be a shapeless lump. When your model is similar in projection to the cast (a little under size to allow for the addition of surface modelling) measure the distance from the board (at some definite point) to the tip of the nose you are copying, and transfer this to the clay, fixing the measurement with a peg of wood. Correct this measurement by others taken from the other side, from the

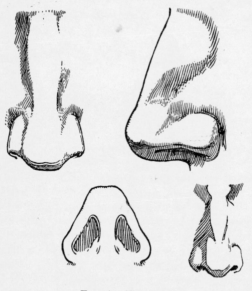

bridge of the nose, from the nostrils, and any other convenient points. When you are satisfied that the point is correctly found, build the clay around the peg until it is firm and steady. Another peg at the bridge of the nose will be sufficient. Continue the building - up, paying careful attention to the large planes and surfaces, which should be marked on the clay trenchantly and vigorously. The first stage should be full of movement and energy. The twists and curves in the surface and the broad flat planes must be emphatic and vigorous. Study your work from the profile, from below, above, and in fact from every possible

FIG. 6.—The Nose.

point of view. Note the curve of the nostrils from below, in profile, and from the side. Let the light play over the surface of the cast, by changing its position with regard to the light, and get a clear, definite idea of the forms that make up the nose. For unless your mental grasp is clear and definite, your modelling can never be other than vacillating and undecided. Don't attempt to smooth the surface, for this will never give you anything worth having, but analyse and then proceed with decision to reproduce the forms in clay. A glance at Fig. 6 and Plate IV. (*a*) will give you some idea of the mode of procedure. These illustrations and a careful reference to the cast before you will be of greater value than any amount of verbal instruction. When the whole of the model has been vigorously roughed in, and the projections and general lines are correct, it is time to attempt finishing. For this stage, clay rather softer than that used in building-up should be employed, and should be spread as a thin skin over the underlying forms, veiling but not obliterating. Note particularly the narrow planes that occur at the base of the hollows. There are no sharp crevices, but a shallow space, the bottom of which is rounded, giving a rich full shadow, rather than a thin, meagre, black scratch. In his analysis the student will be led to enquire into the anatomical structure which is responsible for the forms. He will find that the nose is partly bone and partly cartilage, with thin sheets of muscle overlying them. The nasal bones form the bridge, supported on either side by the ascending processes of the superior maxillary. Below the bridge, the nose is composed of cartilage and muscle. Plate IV. (*a*) illustrates the first stage in building-up, and Plate IV. (*b*) the second stage. The final stage is the spreading of the soft clay over the forms to soften and blend them together.

The Mouth.—Having modelled the nose we next turn our attention to the mouth. The materials and tools are exactly the same as for the nose, and the method of procedure is also similar. The main facts to be noted are the three lobes composing the upper lip, and the two that determine the modelling in the lower (Fig. 7). The twist in the planes surrounding the mouth, particularly at the corners, should be carefully realised or the lips will lack mobility. Having built up the mass of clay until the correct projection is arrived at (somewhat below the actual bulk to allow for surface modelling), measure carefully from various points to the central

FIG. 7.—The Mouth.

lobe of the upper lip, transferring the measurements to the clay and fixing with a wooden peg. A line strongly incised should then be drawn to mark the division between the lips. Now take the distance from corner to corner, and also from other points to the corners until you are satisfied that these important depressions are correctly placed. Build up the chin and fix its position by means of a peg. The modelling of the lips should now be tackled by laying on balls of clay, as nearly as possible the shape and size of the lobes. Study the work from the profile, from above, from below, from every point of view, until you feel certain that your modelling is correct (Plate IV. (*c*)). The twist of the planes surrounding the mouth must now be vigorously rendered, keeping them strong and full of movement. Do not bring the work up to the full size at this stage, but allow a little for surface modelling. The line between the red portion of the lips and the lighter parts should next be drawn. At the end of the first stage the work should contain all the broad planes and essential forms, but more trenchant and emphatic than in the finished stage (Plate IV. (*d*)).

If there is any tendency to vagueness and indecision now, the finishing will still further smooth out the life, leaving it empty and flaccid. Having built up a vigorous rendering of the essential forms, the final stage is to blend and veil with a thin skin of soft clay. This clay to be used for finishing should be soft enough to spread over the clay below without disturbing it in any way. Again, pay great attention to the subtle planes that occur between the main masses, for these hollows and the delicate bridging thereof are as important as the realisation of the large forms. The finishing requires quite as much skill and care as the analysis of the forms. Many modellings have all the life smoothed out of them in this last stage, even though they were vigorous enough at an earlier stage. The mouth is mainly composed of muscle, though the prominence of the chin depends upon the projecting lower jaw. The lips are curved outwards from corner to corner, which projection is caused by the curve of the upper and lower jaw, and by the teeth. The upper lip has a median furrow terminating in the median lobe or prominence of the red portion of the lip. On either side of this lobe are two slight depressions, with two convex surfaces or lobes which carry the lip in a graceful curve to the corners. The lower lip has a median depression corresponding with the fullness of the lobe on the upper lip, with a lobe on either side running into the angle made by the junction of the upper and lower lips. The play of surface round the corners of the mouth is subtle and full of movement (Fig. 8).

FIG. 8.—The Mouth in Profile.

The Eye.—Having provided yourself with the necessary tools and materials, take a cast of the eye ; and proceed to build up the projections as indicated in the previous instructions. Measure carefully the principal projections and fix them with the pegs of wood. The first thing to note and to aim at reproducing is the bony socket into which the ball is set (Fig. 9 (a)). See that the modelling of this is correct before attempting the eye or the lids. Study from all points of view until you are satisfied that your rendering is as close as you can make it to the original, looking out for the broad surfaces and planes of direction. When the socket is right, roll up a ball of clay similar in size to the eyeball in the cast, and set it in position within the socket (Plate IV. (e)). Consider this ball from every point of view until you are quite sure that it is right in position and projection. It is useless to proceed until the ball is perfectly correct. The next stage is to lay the lids over the ball (Fig. 9 (b), (c), (d), (e)). Press out a flat band of clay, similar in bulk and size to the upper lid, and lay it in position over the orb. Press and model it into shape and then proceed to treat the lower lid in a similar manner (Plate IV. (f)). The advantage of working in this order is that the lids are shaped by the underlying orb, in a similar manner to that obtaining in nature. The ball of the eye lies within the socket, and the thin sheath-like lids are drawn across their contour, being determined by the ball beneath (Fig. 9 (e)). An eye so constructed is infinitely more vital and suggestive of the natural form than one which has been gouged out of a lump of clay. The student is advised to study the skull so as to obtain a clear idea of the bony socket into which the eye is set (Fig. 9 (a)). There is no need to detail here the various bones which enter into the formation of the socket, a glance at the skull (Plate VII.) will be of far greater service than reading a list of names. Note carefully the corners of the eye, particularly the inner, containing the lacrymal fossa (Fig. 9 (b)). The inner corner of the eye is invariably lower than the outer. The treatment of the edges of the lids requires consideration; they should be fairly generous in modelling, as the amount of shade

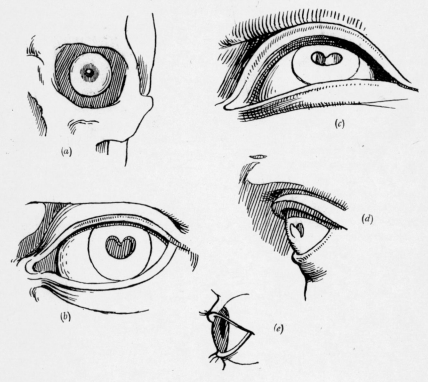

FIG. 9.—The Eye.

cast by the upper lid and the light caught on the lower edge play an important part in the character of the eye. Remember, when modelling a portrait bust, that the lashes help to deepen the shade, and extend the light beyond the actual edges of the lids, giving them a more generous appearance. This must be catered for in the modelling by an added richness in the edges themselves. Fig. 9 (b), (c), (d), and (e) illustrate some of the characteristics of the eye which must be observed in modelling.

CHAPTER III.

MODELLING A BUST FROM LIFE.

Assuming that the student has modelled at least two busts from the antique or the Renaissance, and has built up the skull (Plate VII.) with a view to learning the structures underlying the head, he may be permitted to attempt a portrait bust. In choosing a cast for study it is better to take one in which the forms are well marked and the construction plainly visible. The so-called "Niccolo da Uzzano," and the "Shepherd" by Donatello, and the "Laughing Faun" are splendid examples of clear construction and well-marked form. More can be learned from these than from the smooth, subtle masks that adorn the walls of our art schools. For, beautiful and finished as these masks are, it is a difficult matter for the student, especially in the earlier stages of his study, to trace their construction. Only with a consummate knowledge of form can the beauty of such heads be realised. The student sees only the smooth contours, and in his endeavour to reproduce them, he achieves not merely smoothness but vacuity. It is therefore advisable not to attempt these typically classic heads, but to confine his attention to those which are more obvious in their structures, such as the three busts already mentioned. The method of procedure being exactly similar for all busts, whether from the life or from a cast, it will be sufficient to describe the setting up of a head from the life.

Armature.—Provide yourself with a board about 18 inches square, to the centre of which an upright of about 14 inches high and 2 inches square is fixed. It is an improvement if this upright tapers slightly, say from 2 inches at the base to 1½ inches at the top. The next stage is to fix some piping to this upright to serve as an armature or support for the clay (Fig. 10 (1)). To ensure getting this armature correct in height, take the distance from the pit of the neck to the top of the head on your model. Assuming that the pit of the neck, in your work, comes directly below the top of the upright, you nail your piping to this upright, allowing a little for the covering of clay at the top of the head. Putting one point of the callipers upon the spot fixed for the pit of the neck, the other point should clear the top of the armature by about half an inch. Now fix another piece of piping to the other two faces of the upright (at right angles to the first piece). Nail the piping to the central upright and bend roughly to the shape of head and neck as shown in sketch (Fig. 10 (1)). Keep it well within the outline, as it is not only annoying to be forced to hammer it in later, but it weakens the armature. You will now have a framework narrow at the neck and swelling out slightly in the region of the head. Fix a couple of "butterflies" to provide additional support for the clay as indicated in Fig. 10 (1). Further, nail a strip of wood at right angles to the upright to carry the weight of the clay at the shoulders, and, with copper wire, fasten the two pieces of piping together at the top, where they cross. The armature is now ready.

(18)

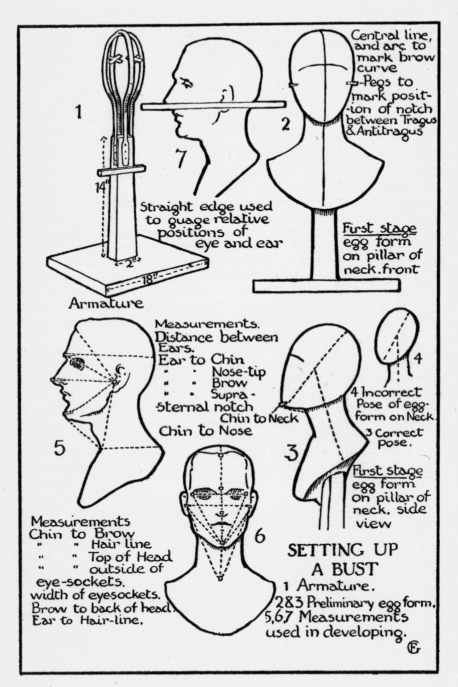

1

14"

2"

18"

Armature

7

Straight edge used
to guage relative
positions of
eye and ear

Central line,
and arc to
mark brow
curve
Pegs to
mark posit-
-ion of notch
between Tragus
& Antitragus

2

First stage
egg form
on pillar of
neck. front

Measurements.
Distance between
Ears.
Ear to Chin
   "   " Nose-tip
   "   " Brow
   "   " Supra-
Sternal notch
          Chin to Neck
Chin to Nose

5

4

4 Incorrect
Pose of egg-
form on Neck.

3 Correct
pose.

3

First stage
egg form
on pillar of
neck. side
view

Measurements
Chin to Brow
   "   " Hair line
   "   " Top of Head
   "   " outside of
eye-sockets.
width of eyesockets.
Brow to back of head.
Ear to Hair-line.

6

SETTING UP
A BUST
1 Armature.
2&3 Preliminary egg form.
5,6,7 Measurements
used in developing.

FIG. 10.

Building-up.—Take some fairly hard clay, roll it between the hands and press well between the piping. Fill up the space here first and gradually build up the clay, pressing well together to exclude the air. Shape into an egg form, quite symmetrical, and set at an angle to the column of the neck (see Fig. 10 (2) and (3), and Plate V. (*a*) and (*b*)). This egg form must be kept below the size of the head as the forms will be added to it, it being, as it were, the core upon which to build up the features. Note carefully from the profile the angle at which the head is set on the neck. The head has a slight tilt backwards, and the neck a forward tilt. The egg form must be similarly posed upon the pillar of clay which represents the neck. Now incise a line in the centre of the egg from top to bottom, and be sure that the shape is evenly balanced on either side of this line, which will serve as a starting-point for our measurements (Fig. 10 and Plate V. (*a*) and (*b*)).

Measurements.—The first measurement might usefully be taken from the Adam's apple to the chin (Fig. 10 (3)). This is to make sure that the chin is sufficiently far from the piping in the neck ; for not only is it irritating to find the armature obtruding itself, but the necessity which arises for hammering the piping further into the clay weakens it, and renders it liable to collapse under the weight of the head. So it is better to allow an inch or so to the actual length from neck to chin, when fixing the position of the latter on your work. Insert a peg of wood at the point fixed for the chin, which then becomes a centre for measuring. The pegs are better if made of fairly hard wood, a little larger than an ordinary match, particularly at the projecting end. The point of the callipers will need to be placed on the peg whilst describing arcs and settling measurements. Cut seven or eight pegs before starting to measure, and they will be ready when you need them. Build up around the peg marking the projection of the chin, and make it secure. It may then be used as a starting-point for the series of measurements given below in tabular form.

From chin to brow.—Place one leg of the callipers on the peg at chin and describe an arc (Fig. 10 (2)). This represents the brow line.

From chin to the notch at ear.—Place the leg of the callipers on chin peg and describe an arc. Somewhere on this arc the position of the ear will be found.

From chin to nose.—Insert peg and working from the profile, build up the clay until the peg is secure, and as nearly as you can judge correct in projection. Now, with the head of the model posed similarly to the clay, carefully gauge the line joining nose and ear. This should be done by holding a ruler or other straight edge as shown in Fig. 10 (7). Then hold the straight edge in a similar position with regard to the egg and insert peg at the intersection of the straight edge and the arc previously struck from the chin. Repeat this on the other side.

Distance between ears.—Press the pegs home on either side, marking the ears, taking care that they are each pressed in equally. If the lengths from chin to ear, and from ear to ear are found to be correct, the ears stand a good chance of being in the right position (Fig. 10 (6)).

Now turn the model and work on the profile, building up until the projections are fairly correct—

From ear to tip of nose.

From ear to brow.

From chin to hair line.

PLATE V.

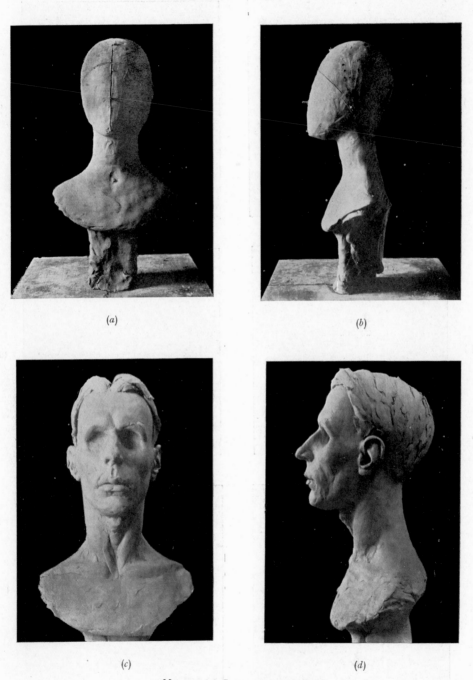

(a)

(b)

(c)

(d)

METHOD OF CONSTRUCTING A BUST.

PLATE VI.

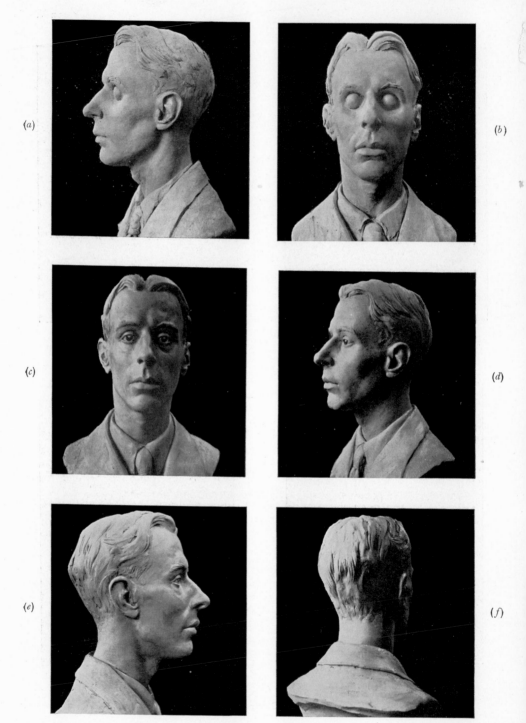

(a)

(b)

(c)

(d)

(e)

(f)

DEVELOPMENT OF A PORTRAIT BUST.

From ear to hair line.

Width at outside of eye-sockets.   Then hollow out the eye-sockets.

Width at zygomatic arches.

From pit of neck to chin.

From pit of neck to ear, on either side.

Next develop the neck and shoulders (Plate V. (a) and (b)).   This will give you the principal measurements, and having fixed them you will have a sound basis to build the head upon.   It is wise to have a board handy, upon which to mark the various lengths, it will save worrying the model unnecessarily.   The first stage of the head should resemble the skull (see Plate VII.)—the angle of the jaw firm and strong, the cheek bones and zygomas well marked, the projection of the nasal bone, and the hollow eye sockets all based on the bony structure (Plate V. (c) and (d)).   The collar-bones and the head of the sternum (pit of the neck) should be realised.   Keep your construction as vigorous as you can, for it is very easy to get it flaccid and empty.   The sterno mastoid (from the mastoid process behind the ear to the head of the sternum) may be placed in position, by laying rolls of clay between the two attachments and working into shape. The mass of the trapezius, with the flat plane lying around the 7th cervical in the centre of the muscle must be built up.   Watch the curving planes caused by the twisting fibres as they pass from the base of the skull forward to the clavicles (Plate V. (c) and (d)).

Pose of Head.—When the column of the neck has been built up and the main forms of the head and shoulders roughed in, the head may be posed.   The work so far has been done with the head facing the front.   An opportunity has been afforded, while the model rested, for noting the way he carried his head.   Every one has a characteristic pose, a particular way of carrying the head which is peculiar to that person.   In a portrait study this pose should be carefully observed, for it aids considerably in the production of a likeness.   The pose decided upon, grasp your study firmly behind the ears, and turn the head into the desired position.   Now devote your attention to the development of the portrait.

Eyes.—The eyes are best constructed by placing balls of clay within the sockets (Plate VI. (a) and (b)).   Study them from below, from above, and from either side until you are satisfied that they lie correctly in the cavities.   The lids should be laid on as flat pieces of clay modelled as nearly as you can judge to size and thickness.   By laying these pieces over the balls they will mould themselves to the contours beneath, even as the eyelids in the model.   The edges of the lids require thought, they should not be too thin, but slightly richer than in nature, for the lashes on the upper lid, help to cast a deeper shadow, while those on the under lid tend to broaden the light caught by the edge.   The dark colour of iris and pupil are suggested by carving a hollow the depth of which is decided by the colour of the eye in the model.   The high light that is invariably present in the eye can be suggested by leaving a small piece projecting from above into the hollow (Plate VI. (c) and (d)).   This point of light is situated just under the greatest projection of the upper lid.   The corners of the eye, inner and outer, must be carefully realised.   The upper lid rises abruptly from the inner corner and sweeps over the ball of the eye to the outer corner (Fig. 9 (b)). The lower lid is somewhat straighter than the upper until it reaches the outer corner, where it sweeps upward to the overlapping upper lid.   The inner corner is somewhat lower than the outer, and also a little in advance, so that the outer corner lies farther back than the inner.   The upper lid folds upon itself, making the line of demarcation between it and the brow much more strongly marked than the junction of the lower lid and the cheek.

The Nose.—The nose is also capable of division into distinct forms.   Above we have the bony parts at the root and the bridge, immediately below which comes the cartilage, with the fleshy part at the tip, and immediately behind the curved wings of the nostrils.   Between the nostrils is the narrow strip of cartilage, the septum, which runs inwards to the upper lip.   The junction here must be closely observed, and it will be seen that there is not a sharp angle, as students so often render it, but a gentle curve (Fig. 6).   The knowledge gained by our previous study of the nose from " David " will stand us in good stead in our present work, for though there is an infinite variety in the shapes and sizes of this organ, they are all based on the main forms so skilfully realised in this detail from Michelangelo's wonderful statue.   A thorough knowledge of this particular nose will be of inestimable value in helping us to appreciate any deviation from the basic type that may occur in the feature we are studying.

The Mouth.—The mouth is capable of considerable movement, playing an important part in the expression ; and the suggestion of mobility attendant thereon is an important factor in the make-up of the mouth.   There is a considerable variety in the thickness of the red or mucous surfaces in different models, but in all cases they are thicker in the middle, with a delicate tapering of their bowed surfaces towards the corners.   The upper lip has three lobes, and the lower two, the central lobe of the upper fitting into the cavity between the two lobes in the lower lip.   The lips, therefore, should be built up with balls of clay of correct size, in imitation of these lobes.   Note the general convexity of the mouth as affected by the teeth, which causes the corners to lie further back than the centre.   Again, the convexity of the planes above and below the mouth, where the upper lip rises to meet the nose, and the lower descends into the depression above the mental eminence, is noteworthy.   The play of surface at the corners of the mouth also demands care and study.   The mass of the chin covers the front portion of the lower jaw, and is sometimes square and angular and sometimes plump and rounded, according to the type of model.

The Jaw Line.—The line of the jaw is continued on either side back to the angle just below the ear (Plate VI. (*d*) and (*e*)).   This, again, may be strongly marked or softly rounded, square or sharply rising, according to type.   Above the angles of the jaw, and immediately in front of the ears, the zygomatic arches are situated, and it is here that the face is widest.   Below the zygomas a depression occurs which is either sharply defined or merely a gentle hollow, depending upon the sex, age, and type of model.   The width between these arches should be measured and transferred to the study (Plate VII. (*a*)).

The Brows.—The brows in the male are usually marked by the frontal sinuses occurring on either side of and above the root of the nose, over which the forehead rises in a smooth plane, curving backwards at the top where the hair veils its form.   The forehead in the female head is smooth and rounded.   Note the planes at the temples, around and behind the eye-sockets, over the malar bones, into the depression that occurs below the zygomas, where the surface rises again over the masseter muscles, dipping suddenly under the line of the jaw to the neck.

The Ears.—The ears are worthy of attention, in fact they demand more than the student is usually prepared to give them.   For unless correctly placed, well drawn, and right in projection your study cannot resemble the model. If the projection is too great, your work will appear too broad, if too little the head will have a pinched look. It is equally dangerous to make them too small, or too large, or to place them too far forward, or too far back. In either of these cases your study will look wrong, and it may puzzle you to ascertain where the fault lies. It often saves a good deal of time, when a head looks wrong, and you are doubtful as to the cause, to test the position, projection, and shape of the ears, for the student is inclined to regard them as of minor import and to treat them accordingly. The junction of the ear with the head, both in front and behind, must be carefully realised. It is fatal to scamp the modelling of these parts, as the result is a lack of homogeneity and completeness, altogether destructive to the character of your portrait. The ear is wholly cartilaginous, and therefore extremely varied in curvature. You will rarely find two models with noses, eyes, or mouths in any way alike, but there is a still more marked variety in the ears.

The Hair.—The hair is always a difficult proposition, it can so easily be made smooth and flaccid, or lumpy and heavy. Study the character of the hair, note whether it is crisply curled, gently waved, or straight and lank. Pay great attention to its main masses and realise these first. Note the way the hair grows and the principal directions in which it turns (Plate VIII. (a) and (b)). Note the way it starts at the crown of the head and radiates from this point, merging in an interesting series of curves with that which grows from the forehead and temples. The blending of the colour of the hair with that of the flesh around the face is a further point to be observed. Unless due attention is paid to this hair line, it will seem as though the head were crowned with an ill-fitting wig. It is a further instance of " losing and finding." A deep undercut shadow merging into a plane which leaves the flesh almost imperceptibly, a sharp touch in one place and a gentle mingling of surfaces elsewhere, will alone give that suggestion of growth which is so essential in a modelling. Draw the general contours, and watch that your minor masses shall be contained within them. Aim at getting the spring and suppleness so characteristic of hair. The texture is suggested by a few well-placed strokes of the modelling tool, or a piece of wood snapped across the grain, and the jagged edge of the fracture used with restraint. The texture is best suggested at the overlapping edges of the masses, and by a judicious breaking up of these and a few incised lines carried across the masses at well-chosen parts, it is possible to suggest the character of hair far more truthfully than by scratching over the whole surface, with finely incised lines. The collar-bones and forms in the neck and shoulders having been built up, the whole head is complete in its big masses. Plate VIII. shows the characteristic massing of hair and beard.

Drawing.—During the process of building-up, the head should be drawn from every point of view (Plate VI. (c), (d), (e), and (f)). Keep the model and your work turning so that you do not spend too long on any one view. Draw as carefully as you are able the contours from each view-point. Each part, as you build it up, should be regarded from the front, from either side, from above, and from below. You must be constantly on the *qui vive*, both mentally and physically, for the task in hand admits of no slackness. Remember that it is all a matter of drawing; your medium is clay and you make the forms instead of outlining them with charcoal or pencil, but it is essentially drawing, and difficult drawing too, for instead of only one contour you must render many. Do not neglect this precaution, for if you do you will lay yourself open for much disappointment. You will probably get a contour beautifully drawn, spending a lot of time and thought upon it, only to find that another point of view proves it to be entirely unrelated to the other parts of the head. Time and labour wasted. It is far better to proceed gradually, to build up every part of the head equally and never to leave a form until you have looked at it from all round.

Finishing.—The head having reached the stage when all the essential forms are built up, and the drawing correct, though somewhat below the actual bulk to allow for finishing, it is time to pull the forms together by adding a thin skin of soft clay. At this stage it should be a vigorous representation of the forms which enter into the make-up of the head, with everything strong and well-defined. The addition of the skin (or thin layer of clay) should veil and refine these trenchant forms, without robbing them of their character. Too often a vigorous work is spoiled in the finishing. The student is so anxious to get his surface smooth, that he loses the drawing, wipes away all the forms, and runs his planes together, until instead of being full of movement and interest, the head resembles one of those effigies used by the hairdresser to display his wigs. In his efforts to smooth the surface, he has produced an empty meaningless one. But he must learn to spread the soft clay over and between the masses in such a manner as to add to the vitality, rather than to detract from it. Between all the projecting forms in the human head, lie depressions full of subtlety. There are no sharp dark crevices, but rather delicate bridges, or soft depressions made up of distinct planes that hold no black shadows, merely subtle tones. The depths of these depressions must be carefully studied, as they are of vital importance to the work. If made too deep they will break up the surface, and rob the head of all semblance of flesh, whereas if too shallow, emptiness and vacuity will result. It is a good plan to test the depths by laying a ruler or straight-edge across the projecting forms, and carefully studying the distance to the base of the hollow. Generally one is surprised at the shallowness thereof. Again, keep your work and the model constantly turning, in order to see the forms in different lights. Have a damp sponge at hand, and with it keep your thumb and fingers moist. Use clay of a softer quality than that of which the underlying forms are built up, for only a thin veil should be spread over them, blending, but not obliterating. Keep your hands clean, also the modelling tools, for it is impossible to model when everything is messed up with clay. In fact, keep your whole work as clean as possible, even the stand upon which the work rests, for it is very distracting to have lumps of clay scattered all over the place.

The Base.—The final consideration is the base. There are various ways of finishing off a bust. Sometimes the neck alone is included, but generally the shoulders enter into the scheme as well. Care and thought are necessary in finishing off the work here and setting it upon the base. Many busts are marred by unsuitable bases. It is impossible to lay down any definite formulas, as different heads demand different treatments of the base. All that can be said is that the base should appear sufficient to support the weight above, or a top-heavy look will result. The base should be an integral part of the work, and not look as though the bust had been perched upon it as an after-thought. Give the base due consideration, then, as an essential part in the scheme, and be quite sure that it looks adequate to support the upper part. Plate IX.

PLATE VII.

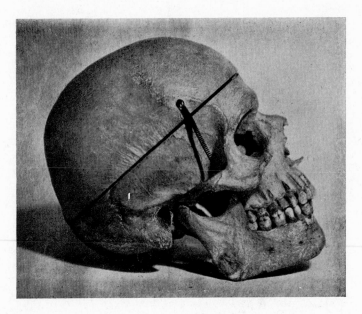

(a)

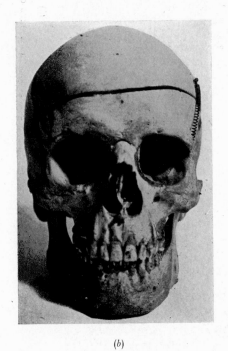

(b)

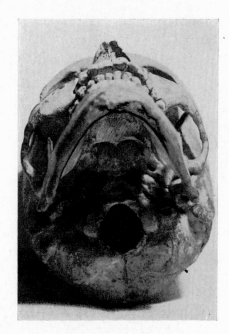

(c)

THE HUMAN SKULL.

PLATE VIII.

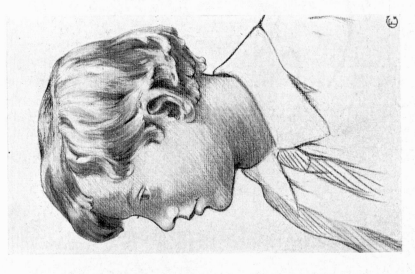

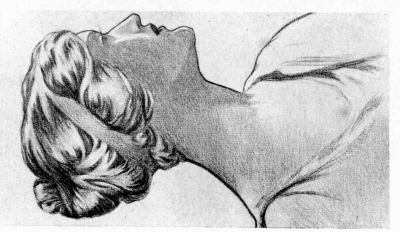

(a)　　　　　(b)　　　　　(c)

SCULPTURESQUE STUDIES OF HAIR AND BEARD.

PLATE IX.

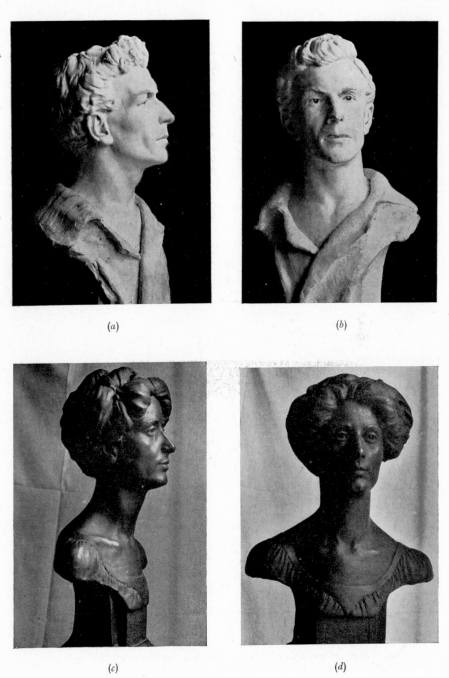

(a)

(b)

(c)

(d)

PORTRAIT BUSTS.

PLATE X.

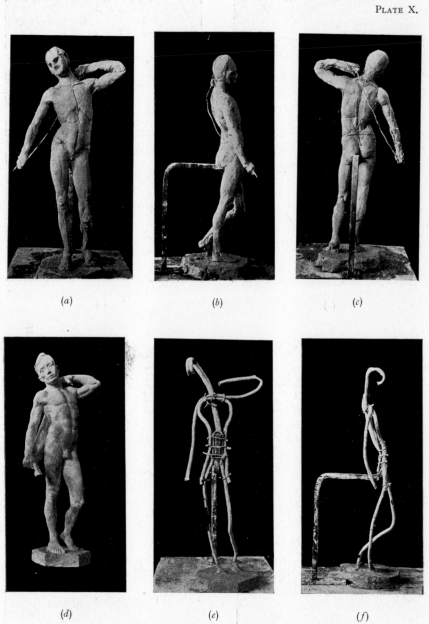

(a) (b) (c)

(d) (e) (f)

ARMATURE FOR THE DEVELOPMENT OF A STUDY FROM LIFE.

(*a*) and (*b*) illustrates a bust with crisp curling hair and also the way in which it radiates from the crown. Plate IX. (*c*) and (*d*) shows a female bust with big, decorative masses of hair and greater subtlety of modelling than in the male heads. The subjects on Plate VIII. were drawn with a view to showing the sculpturesque massing of hair on the female head, on a child's head, and in the masculine beard.

CHAPTER IV.

MODELLING THE FIGURE FROM LIFE.

THERE is some diversity of opinion as to when the student should be allowed to attempt to model the human figure. But as soon as some familiarity with the clay, combined with a knowledge of anatomy, and of the figure by means of drawing, has been acquired, there is no reason why the student should not attempt to model the figure from life. The difficulties he will then meet, and his efforts to overcome them, will, if properly directed, teach him more about the human body than he is likely to learn in any other way. It is a good plan to have a study from the antique going in conjunction with the study from the life. The due importance given to essentials and the breadth of treatment in these idealised figures cannot fail to assist the student in the formation of his style. It is also calculated to assist him in overcoming the difficulties that will arise in his work from the life, for having studied the various forms in the antique figure, he will approach similar forms in the living model with greater confidence. Needless to say, a knowledge of anatomy is indispensable, and if the student is not already familiar with this subject he will find as he proceeds, how seriously his lack of knowledge retards his progress. The knowledge of anatomy, rightly applied, enables one to model a figure in which the forms are not only correct, but full of life and movement. The danger is, otherwise, that the limbs will appear as though they had been turned on a lathe, while the trunk and head are smooth, empty, and uninteresting. Of course there is a risk also to be guarded against, of putting in too much anatomy, and producing a Hercules when you wished to model an Apollo. But the fault is usually the other way, as the study of anatomy requires application and a certain amount of labour. " Copy the model." " Copy the model as you see it," we hear the various authorities iterating and reiterating. Splendid advice, the best possible, if accompanied by an explanation. For it is not exactly copying, but translating. The model is composed of bone, muscle, tendon, cartilage, fatty substance, skin and hair : our medium is clay, and only clay. The model again has the advantage of delicately varied colour : our medium is uniform in tint. So that whilst we copy as closely as we are able, there yet enters into the work an element of translation and suggestion. We render the forms to the best of our ability, and endeavour to get the appearance presented by the model in our figure. But it is rendering, and not wholly copying. The hair, for instance : it would be hopeless to attempt modelling the fine hairs of which the mass is composed, so we copy the mass in its broad general planes and suggest the texture. The eyes, again, are suggested by hollowing out a cavity, the depth of which gives a shadow approaching as nearly as possible the tone of the pupil and iris. The same translation to a greater or lesser degree is applied to the whole figure. It is here particularly that the

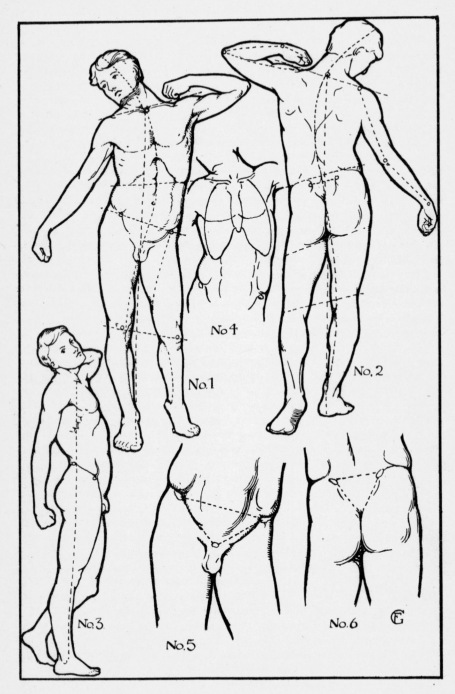

FIG. 11.—The Selected Pose.

knowledge of anatomy and the study of the antique will afford skill and confidence.

Suggestion of Movement.—One of the chief difficulties encountered by the student is in the conveyance of that suggestion of life and movement which the human figure (however static the pose) always possesses. Though the model may be rigidly based, both feet firmly planted, arms straight down, and head facing the front, there is still that suggestion of a possibility of movement, of a quick, easy alteration of pose, combined with a mobility in every part, that is so difficult to render in clay. To the student this lightness and freedom of movement is one of the greatest obstacles presented in modelling the figure. Too often one sees clay figures so stiff and wooden, so apparently incapable of movement, that they bear a ludicrous resemblance to the Dutch dolls that amused us in our infancy. It is by no means an easy task for the instructor, on his rounds, to infuse life into so stiff an effigy. Much of this desirable suggestion of life and movement lies in the correct rendering of form and contour, drawing, in fact, for unless the shapes and planes are realised, stiffness and rigidity are inevitable, but by choosing a pose in which there is contrast of line and plane the task is simplified considerably.

The Pose.—The superiority of a free, easy pose over a stiff rigid one is well illustrated in the work of the best Greek period as compared with that of the earlier archaic period. The student is therefore advised to choose a pose which is loose and easy in itself as it gives greater scope for freedom and ease in treatment. If the weight of the figure is borne by one leg, whilst the other hangs loose, the difference between the legs at once affords a contrast which makes for movement. Besides which the twist of the pelvis, and furthermore of the torso, as the body bends to maintain its equilibrium, together with the droop of the shoulder on the side of the standing leg, will, if realised and truthfully rendered, assist materially in suggesting movement. A pose such as the one chosen for demonstration on Fig. 11 and Plate X. should therefore be adopted for a start.

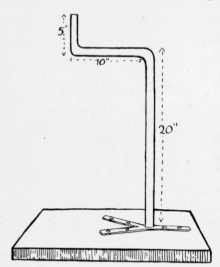

FIG. 12.—A Simple Armature.

The Armature.—Having settled the pose (which must to some extent depend on the model we are working from, for some models look well in a pose which in another becomes so uninteresting that we have no desire to copy it), the armature or framework must be constructed. Procure an iron support (Fig. 12) and screw firmly to a stout board about 18 inches square, to the underside of which two strong battens have been fastened (across the grain) to prevent it from warping. This iron support should be about 20 inches by 10 inches by 5 inches for a half life-size figure, which is the most convenient size for a study, being large enough to enable us to copy the forms in the model

without niggling, but not too large for comfortable handling.   Life-size studies
should certainly be attempted later, but at first it is well not to overtax our
strength and ability.

  The Modelling Stand.—A modelling stand (Fig. 13) with a revolving
top is necessary for working upon.   This should be about 40 inches high, and
if the board at the top is made so that it may be raised or lowered at will, it
adds to its usefulness.   The model must also be posed on a revolving " throne "
raised some 18 inches from the floor of the studio.   The " armature " or skeleton
upon which our clay figure is built is constructed of lead or " Compo " piping,
such as the plumber uses (Fig. 14).   This piping is strong enough to support

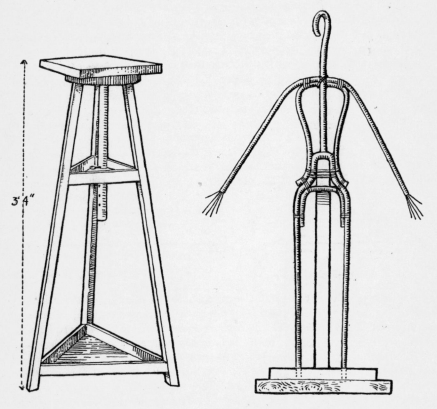

FIG. 13.—A Modelling Stand.   FIG. 14.—The Finished Armature.

the weight of the clay, and at the same time pliable enough to allow us to bend
it to the curves of the figure.   Plate X. (*e*) and (*f*) give an idea of the framework
to be constructed.   For binding the piping together and also to the iron support
copper wire should be used, as iron wire is apt to rust and to mark the clay with
an objectionable stain.   Anneal the wire before using as otherwise it is apt to
snap when being tightened.   Our figure being half life-size, it will be necessary
to construct a reducing scale as follows.

  Scale.—Procure a fairly large board and draw a line about 3 feet long down
one side.   Take half the height of the model (from the pubic arch to the ground,
or top of the head) in your callipers, and placing one leg at the end of the line,

describe an arc (Fig. 15, B-C). If a small stud is embedded in the board at the end of the line A it will materially assist in fixing the end of the callipers on the correct point, as a number of measurements will be taken and the point is liable to get obliterated. Now take half the height of your framework in the callipers, and, with one leg resting on B, cut off the arc at C. Draw a line from point A through this intersection at C, and the scale is ready for use. All future reductions are made from the model by placing one leg of the callipers on A and describing an arc to intersect lines AB and AC. The required measurement is the length of the arc between its intersections with lines AB and AC. It is a good plan to continue the arc some distance beyond the intersecting line, and to write upon it the measurement it represents. This will save worrying the model unnecessarily, and is useful for testing measurements when the model is not available. A somewhat similar scale is used for enlarging (Fig. 16). Describe an arc of convenient radius, ABC, with the same radius mark off distance BD, and with AD as radius describe arc DE. Take the height of the model, or half the height if preferred, and transfer it to BC. Draw a line through C, cutting the arc DE at E. The measurements taken from the model are then marked on the arc BC, and a line drawn through the intersection until it cuts the arc DE. This is the enlarged measurement required,

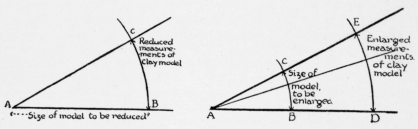

FIG. 15.—Reducing Scale.   FIG. 16.—Enlarging Scale.

being twice the size of the first one. Should a scale for enlarging three times be required the distance AB is marked three times along the line, for enlarging four times the distance is marked four times, and so on. Having prepared the armature and the scale (for reducing in this case) place the former on the modelling stand, and the board upon which the scale is drawn, in a convenient position near at hand. Pose the model on the " throne " and take up your position where you can see the whole figure at a glance. Study the pose carefully, noting the lines and planes of contrast, so that when the model tires, and begins to relax, there shall be less danger of your work following suit. Pay attention to the salient points and give due emphasis to them.

Posing the Armature.—The framework of piping is now bent to take the main curves of the pose. Turn the model until he is directly facing you, and study the line from the pit of the neck through the thorax, over the abdomen, and down the standing leg to the ankle (No. 1, Fig. 11). In a standing pose where the figure has no external support the pit of the neck will be vertically over the inner ankle of the standing leg. If the figure stands equally on both legs a vertical line from the pit of the neck will fall midway between the two feet. If this line is not observed there will be a lack of equilibrium in the appearance of your figure. Try this carefully with your plumb-line, and then turn your attention to the armature. Settle the position of the pit of the neck (suprasternal fossa) and bend your piping until the main central line is similar to that in the model. Test with the plumb-line and embed the piping of the standing leg in the clay at the base (Plate X. (e)). It is advisable to keep the base about 3 inches thick, so that should you require a little more length in the legs, you can cut the base away instead of altering the whole figure. Now turn the model and study the back view in the same way (No. 2, Fig. 11), again testing with the plumb-line. The back (posterior) line should correspond with the front (anterior) line. Next turn to the side view and fit the piping to the main lines from this view (Plate X. (f)). When fixing the armature of the bent leg, scale the distance between the feet and watch the line carefully with regard to the other leg. In a pose such as the one chosen for demonstration the following points should be observed. The figure is balanced upon the right leg, practically the whole weight resting thereon. The pelvis is therefore raised on the right side, as the femur and tibia, being in a vertical line, maintain their entire length. On the left side the ilium drops because the left leg is pendant, both the thigh and leg being bent. A line drawn through the two subcutaneous points of the iliac bones (the anterior superior iliac spines) will therefore be inclined downwards from right to left (No. 1, Fig. 11). The body above the hips will curve towards the side of the standing leg (right side) to maintain its equilibrium, and in so doing will depress the right shoulder (No. 1, Fig. 11). This gives us another inclined line, the line of the shoulders, but this time inclined in the opposite direction ; the left shoulder is up and the right down, so the line slopes downwards from left to right. Besides this inclination downwards, there is a further inclination to be noted in the planes of the shoulders and pelvis, a slope from back to front. The anterior superior iliac spine on the right side of the figure is in advance of the spine on the left side, hence the plane of the pelvis is inclined backwards from right to left. The shoulders give us a plane which is in direct contrast to this, for the left shoulder comes forward whilst the right recedes. The shoulders are therefore inclined backwards from left to right (No. 3, Fig. 11). We are thus provided with two lines of contrast and two planes of contrast. The next parts to consider are the patellas. A line drawn between these will slope downwards from the right (standing leg) to the left (bent leg) and the left knee is in advance of the right one. The left foot lies behind the right, whilst the head is inclined towards the standing leg. Turning to the back view we find similar lines and planes of contrast (No. 2, Fig. 11). The posterior spines of the pelvis contrast with the shoulders, and the plane at the upper part is opposed to that of the lower part ; but enough has been said to indicate to the student the essential lines and planes to be looked for when setting up the figure. The front, back, and side views have been considered separately here, but merely because it was more convenient to do so ; when arranging your armature it is advisable to get a clear grasp of the pose from each standpoint, so that the piping may be bent with confidence. For the fingers, copper wires must be inserted into the end of the arm pipes, and secured by nipping the piping with the pliers.

Building-up—First Stage.—When you are satisfied with the lines of the armature, which should suggest in skeleton form the pose of the figure, it is time to commence putting on the clay. This should be moderately hard, and must be pressed well together round the framework. Roll the clay between the hands before applying, as this makes it more homogeneous and easy to handle. See that no air spaces are left, and that the whole is well knit together, or later on you will find your work falling to pieces.   With this fairly hard clay cover the whole of the piping, and, keeping it very thin in bulk, shape it roughly to the main forms of the figure, paying particular attention to the principal lines and planes of contrast.   On this coating of clay draw firmly the chief lines of the figure, front and back (see Plate X. (*a*) and (*c*)).   Good vigorous curves are advisable as the tendency is always to slide back towards stiff vertical lines. Use the plumb-line to help in gauging these lines.

Measurements.—The next stage is to take a series of measurements, and to fix them in the clay by means of small wooden pegs.   These pegs should be slightly larger than a match, and are better if made of hard wood.   The projecting end must be large enough to rest one point of the callipers upon.   Prepare a number of pegs before commencing to measure.   A thin strip of wood embedded in the clay plinth between the feet gives a firm foundation from which to commence measuring.   A series of measurements are given in tabular form, as a systematic procedure is better than working in a haphazard fashion.

1. Plinth (under foot of standing leg) to patella.
2. Patella to anterior superior iliac spine.   (In a well-proportioned figure these two distances will coincide.   See Fig. 11, Plate X. (*a*), (*b*), (*c*).)
3. Plinth to iliac spine.   (If this agrees with the point previously fixed we may assume that it is fairly correct ; it should be further tested by plumbing through the centre of patella, and estimating the distance between this vertical line and the spine.)
4. Distance between anterior iliac spines.   (Before fixing the pegs to represent these points, gauge by means of a straight-edge the angle made by a line joining them.)
5. Iliac spine to patella of bent leg.
6. Patella to base of great toe on bent leg.
7. Iliac process of standing leg to pit of neck.
8. Iliac process of bent leg to pit of neck.
9. Distance between anterior and posterior iliac spines, right side.
10. Distance between anterior and posterior iliac spines, left side.
11. Distance between posterior spines (again using straight edge to gauge the inclination of the line joining them).
12. Suprasternal notch to 7th cervical vertebrae.
13. Posterior superior spine of standing leg to 7th cervical.
14. Posterior superior spine of bent leg to 7th cervical.
15. Acromion process to olecranon process, bent arm.
16. Olecranon process to end of ulna, bent arm.
17. Acromion process to olecranon process, straight arm.
18. Olecranon process to end of ulna, straight arm.
19. Suprasternal notch to ear.
20. Suprasternal notch to top of head.

The measurements for the head are dealt with in the section devoted to modelling the bust.   This series of measurements taken from bony prominence must be carefully scaled, tested, and fixed on the clay by means of the small pegs of wood.   Write each measurement on the scale for future reference. It is not safe to rely on measurements taken between fleshy portions of the model, as they are variable. Proceed so far systematically, working in the order suggested, but when developing the figure you may take as many other measurements as you require, using as far as possible the bony structure, as it is less liable to change. Each peg should be well supported with clay, or pressed home as the case may be, until it marks the correct position and projection of the point it indicates. It should be allowed to project slightly from the surface of the clay, distinctly visible, until the final stage, when it may be pressed in and the hole smoothed over. The clay now bears a slender resemblance to the pose of the model, with the principal points in the structure indicated by pegs.

Building-up—Second Stage.—The next step is to develop the work by laying on the various forms with due regard for the muscles and the planes of direction. The student will find a knowledge of anatomy indispensable at this juncture, for knowing the muscles, their shapes, actions, and directions of fibres, he can render with greater confidence and vitality the forms they are responsible for. Needless to say, the skeleton is a necessity for reference, so much depends on the bones, whilst a good anatomical figure will prove invaluable. In the human figure you will find forms so subtle, that unless the requisite knowledge is brought to bear upon them, they will appear vague and indeterminate. Trite, but true is the statement, "The eye only sees that which it brings the power to see." Know and you will see, doubt and you will flounder. The human figure is marvellously subtle ; delicate tints and textures tend to veil the construction, a superficial layer of fatty tissue further modifies it, and often the forms will remain invisible until a strong side light is brought to bear on the model, when projections and depressions will leap into view which previously were unsuspected. Search, analyse, watch. Study the model in all his attitudes ; as he moves to and from the " throne " and when he rests. Endeavour to trace the muscles and see how they play their parts in the movements of the body. For without precise knowledge you can never hope to translate those subtle forms and movements. I do not say copy, for, as previously stated, it is not so much copying as translating. Were it possible to represent exactly the forms in the model, with each plane and muscle projecting or receding from surrounding forms, to exactly the same extent as in the model, with nothing emphasised, nothing restrained, the result, lacking as it must the variety of colour and texture of the flesh, would be very disappointing. The clay, absolutely uniform in tint, and texture also, unless they are suggested by the modeller, would in this exact copy give but a poor idea of the living figure. Vitality, life, and mobility, animate the human body, and however still it may be, it never lacks this suggestion of movement and life. In our work we fix the movement, we petrify it once and for all time, and the rigidity of clay, bronze or stone, can only be counteracted by treating it vigorously and sculpturesquely. By emphasis here, subordination there, by trenchant treatment in one place, and suavity in another, we strive to suggest a living being, capable of movement, who has settled for a moment into a graceful attitude, but is by no means frozen there, and who will shortly change to some other attitude, equally graceful and easy. It may seem that undue preponderance is given to the necessity for translation, for treating the figure in such a manner as to suit it to clay, especially when by so doing we are flying in the face of those who reiterate " Copy the model." But I think that a careful study of Greek, Renaissance, and good modern sculpture, will impress upon the student the need

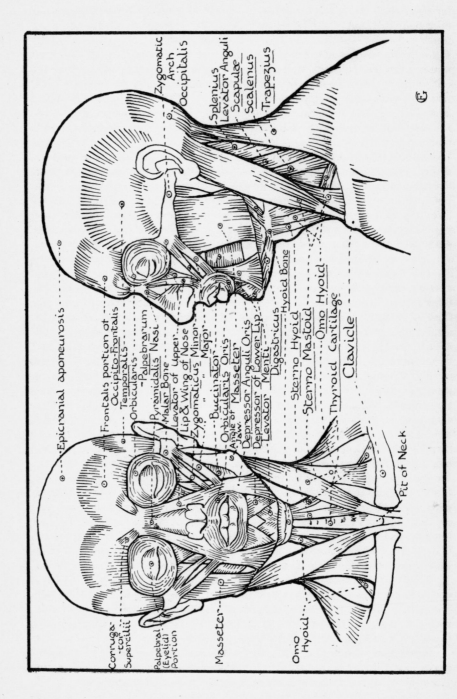

FIG. 17.—Head and Neck Muscles.

for translating rather than copying.   We talk so glibly of idealising, we speak
of the subtle beauty of Phidias and the titanic energy of Michelangelo, admitting thereby, the subordination of certain qualities to emphasise others.
But only to these great ones in art is such treatment allowed ; the student must
not attempt it.   He may study, he may even copy the works of the masters,
but when it comes to life-work we merely repeat " Copy the model."   And
really, there can be no better advice, provided we explain how the model should
be copied.   Learn from the model and stick to facts as far as possible, but at
the same time let us learn how to treat these facts.   Let us see how the masters
have rendered them, and so learn the technique of sculpture.   The student
will find as he goes along that he will emphasise some parts, and subordinate
others ; he will idealise, perhaps unconsciously, but as he develops his technical
skill and his individuality he will idealise still more.   " Art is art because it is
not Nature," says Goethe.   Copy the model but copy it intelligently.   Get a
clear idea of the construction of the human figure, and in time you may use it
with all the freedom and facility of a Michelangelo.   Take the bony structure,
search out its influence on the forms, where and how it is capable of movement,
where it is subcutaneous, and how it determines the proportions of the figure.

The Skull.—The head and face are moulded by the skull.   The general
contour, modified by the hair and flesh, is really the contour of the skull.   The
brow is modelled by the underlying bone, over which is stretched but a thin
sheet of muscle.   The eye-sockets into which the ball is set, determines the
forms about the eye.   The malar bones and zygomatic arches are responsible
for the cheeks, and the lower jaw moulds the chin and lower part of the face
back to the ear.   The nose is built upon the nasal bones (Fig. 17).   The head
is uplifted by the cervical vertebrae, the 7th of which has a prominent spine
projecting from the diamond-shaped plane lying between the fibrous parts of
the trapezius at the back of the neck (Figs. 19 and 22).   The column of the
neck is based upon the clavicles in front and the spines of the scapulas behind.
The upper part of the trunk is built around the thorax, or cage of ribs which
spring from the twelve dorsal vertebrae behind, and, except for the two lower
ones, are attached either directly or indirectly to the sternum in front (Fig. 18).
The two lower ones are free in the muscles of the trunk at their anterior ends.
Study carefully the form of the thorax, note its slightly conical, barrel-shaped
cage, across the upper portion of which lie the pectorals, whilst the lower part
provides support to the serratus magnus, external oblique, and rectus abdominis in front, and behind to the latissimus dorsi, etc. (Fig. 19).   The collar
bones, attached to the head of the sternum, take a double curve outwards
to the shoulders, and help in the formation of the general mass of the thorax.
At the back the trapezius veils the upper part of the thorax, which is further
obscured by the scapulas (Fig. 21).   Below this, however, its rounded barrel-
shaped contour may be discerned beneath the fibres of the latissimus dorsi,
with the spines of the dorsal vertebrae more or less distinctly visible, according
to the pose and muscular development of the model (Fig. 19).

Movement of Thorax.—It will readily be understood, after studying the
construction of the thorax, why the range of movement in this region is limited.
The cage of ribs is more or less compact, hence the vertebral column in the
dorsal region is capable of but little, if any, movement, which takes place in the
lumber and cervical regions particularly, where the vertebræ are set in mobile
muscles, which leave the movements practically unhampered (Figs. 18 and 19).

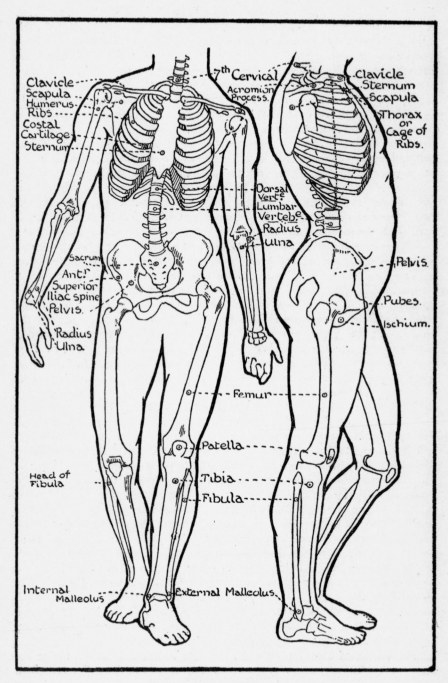

FIG. 18.—Skeleton.

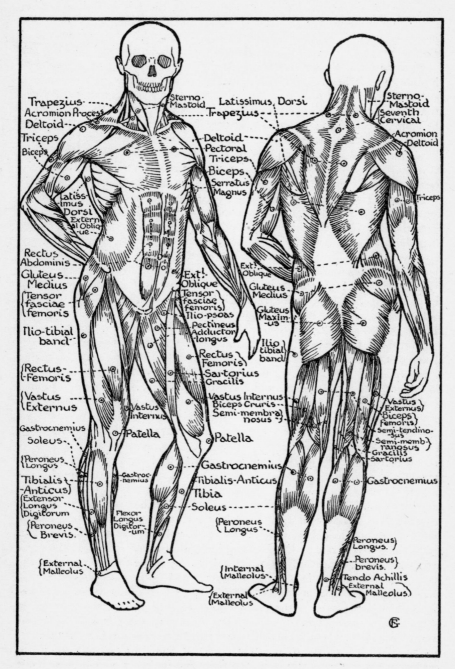

FIG. 19.—Muscles of the Figure.

It follows, therefore, that when the figure bends, the principal change takes place in the forms around the lumbar region ; in the thoracic or dorsal portion the alteration is so slight as to be practically negligible. The movements of the head affect the cervical part of the vertebral column alone.

Symmetrical Mass of Thorax.—In building up the figure the mass of the thorax must be arranged symmetrically on either side of the centre line, back and front, as we have seen how constant is the general form of this cage. But, directly below, there may be a considerable difference in the two sides of the figure, as on one side the muscles may be compressed and on the other stretched between the lower border of the thorax and the iliac spine. The pose chosen for demonstration is an illustration of this difference (Fig. 11 and Plate X.). Note the uniform symmetry of the upper part, contrasted with the difference in length and bulk on either side between the ribs and the pelvis.

Pelvis.—The pelvis, again, is important, most important, as it gives the key to the pose. If the iliac spines, anterior and posterior, are horizontal, we know that the figure rests evenly on both legs. If, however, the lines joining them lie in an oblique direction, we can see at once that the weight is on one leg only, with the other leg relaxed. There are two triangles, one in front and the other behind, that are worthy of consideration. In front the base of the triangle is formed by the two anterior iliac spines, whilst the apex is formed by the pubic spine. The posterior triangle is formed by the iliac spines in this part and the sacrum. Both these triangles are apex downwards, and it is essential that they should be correctly placed in the modelling (Fig. 11, Nos. 5 and 6).

Vertebral Column.—The vertebral column which is formed of cylindrical bones, set one above the other, with a pad of cartilage between, is capable of movement in the backward, forward, and lateral directions, limited in the dorsal, and free in the lumbar and cervical regions (Fig. 18). Seen in profile, it will be noted that the front of the trunk is convex, while the back, which extends both lower and higher than the front, is a double reverse curve, convex above, concave in the small of the back, and convex again at the buttocks. The main lines of direction should be observed : the upper part slopes downwards from back to front, the middle or abdominal slightly backwards, and the lower or pelvic more distinctly backwards (see Fig. 23). This applies more particularly to the erect figure, as considerable modifications take place when the body bends forward. The upper portion is built around the bony thorax, the middle mass is mainly muscle with the vertebral column as the only bone, and the lower part is based on the pelvis, which is, however, well covered with muscle (Fig. 25). The femur is mainly deep seated, being subcutaneous only at the great trochanter, and at the condyles, which help to determine the forms around the knee (Fig. 18). The tibia plays an important part in the modelling of the leg, the curve of the skin being formed entirely by the subcutaneous surface of the bone which terminates in the protuberance or malleolus of the inner ankle (Figs. 20-24). The fibula comes to the surface at its head, and its lower end forms the outer ankle or malleolus. The patella or knee-cap is subcutaneous, and quite distinct on the front of the knee. It should be carefully studied in conjunction with the muscles attached to it, and the short tendon by which it is fastened to the tibia. Its movements as it slides in the groove of the lower end of the condyles of the femur, whilst maintaining its position with regard to the tibia, are important in the modelling of the leg (Figs. 20, 24).

The Foot.—The bones of the foot should be noted, the mass of the tarsal

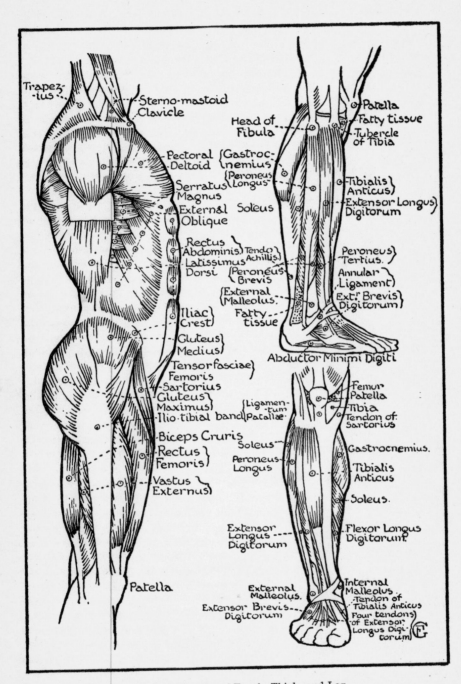

FIG. 20.—Muscles of Trunk, Thigh and Leg.

bones and the long metatarsals and phalanges being the block form upon which the foot is based. The os calcis, or heel bone, projects behind and affords attachment for the tendon Achilles (Fig. 24). In the arm the humerus is well covered, coming to the surface only at the elbow, but here its condyles have a decided effect upon the surface forms (Fig. 27). The ulna gives the sharp protuberance at the elbow which is formed by the olecranon process, after which the bone may be traced by a slight depression down to the wrist on the side of the little finger (Figs. 26 and 27). The carpal bones forming the wrist, and the metacarpal, and the phalanges upon which the hand is built should receive attention. From the above brief sketch some idea of the importance of the skeleton, as a determinant of form and proportion, may be gathered. It also provides attachments for the muscles, and affords leverage for the various movements of the body.

Muscles.—The muscles are illustrated in Figs. 17, 19, 20, 21, 22, 24, 25, and 26. How the muscles act, and how they affect the surface forms when in action is too wide a subject to be properly dealt with here, but a few of the more important points may be noted in passing. It has already been noticed that the thorax is balanced symmetrically on either side of the central line. The muscles covering the cage of ribs lie in fairly close contact with the bones, so it is essential to get the bony mass true in shape before laying on the muscles.

The Pectorals.—Across the chest lie the pectoral muscles, swelling out on either side of the sternum, which is subcutaneous and so forms the depression down the centre line (Fig. 21). The clay should be laid on in the direction of the fibres, which radiate from the sternum and clavicle outwards, over the armpit to the shaft of the humerus. The deltoid, a triangular shaped muscle crowning the shoulder, lies on the outer side of the pectoral, where a slight depression marks the space between the two muscles (Fig. 22). Here, again, the radiation of the fibres between its origin at the scapular spine and the outer third of the clavicle, and its attachment to the deltoid impression on the shaft of the humerus should be observed when laying on the clay. The sweep of the planes bordering the arm-pit, for which these two muscles are accountable, must be realised, as they give a fine play of surface, and suggest vitality.

Rectus abdominis, Serratus magnus, External Oblique.—Below the pectorals lie the rectus abdominis, the serratus magnus, and the external oblique (Figs. 21 and 22). The abdominal muscle is divided vertically by the linea alba, and horizontally by the lineæ transversæ. These divide the muscle into separate bunches of fibres, and afford opportunity for some rich swelling forms. By giving due emphasis to the depression which occurs between the rectus and the external oblique at the outer extremity of the thoracic arch, valuable contrast is afforded to the full forms of the rectus, adding life and movement to the torso. The external oblique arises from the lower eight ribs by a series of slips, the upper four or five of which interdigitate with corresponding slips of the serratus magnus (Fig. 21). These interdigitations are arranged in a curved line starting just below the nipple and passing backwards to the latissimus dorsi. In front the external oblique is attached to the aponeurosis of the abdomen, which is responsible for the depression that occurs between the rectus abdominis and the external oblique. The front of the torso affords scope for rich and varied modelling. The fullness of the muscles, the hard flat plane of the sternum, the finger-like slips of the serratus interdigitating with the oblique muscle ; the ribs suggested rather than insisted upon ; the breaking up

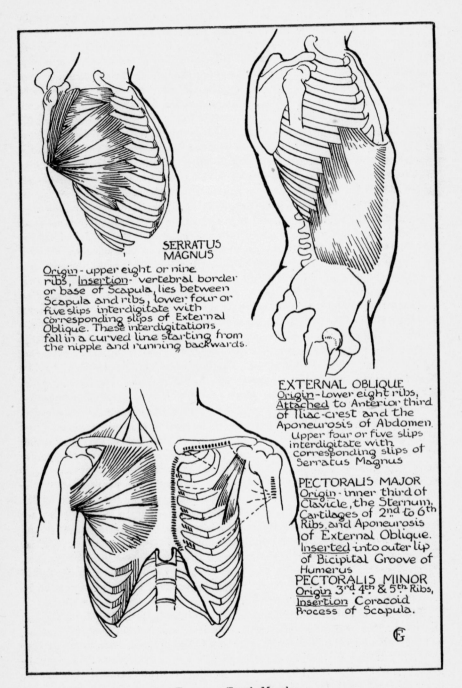

SERRATUS MAGNUS

Origin - upper eight or nine ribs, Insertion - vertebral border or base of Scapula, lies between Scapula and ribs, lower four or five slips interdigitate with corresponding slips of External Oblique. These interdigitations fall in a curved line starting from the nipple and running backwards.

EXTERNAL OBLIQUE
Origin - Lower eight ribs, Attached to Anterior third of Iliac-crest and the Aponeurosis of Abdomen. Upper four or five slips interdigitate with corresponding slips of Serratus Magnus

PECTORALIS MAJOR
Origin - inner third of Clavicle, the Sternum, Cartilages of 2nd to 6th Ribs, and Aponeurosis of External Oblique. Inserted into outer lip of Bicipital Groove of Humerus

PECTORALIS MINOR
Origin 3rd 4th & 5th Ribs, Insertion Coracoid Process of Scapula.

FIG. 21.—Trunk Muscles.

of the abdominal muscle with a deeper depression at the umbilicus, and the
bony spines of the anterior iliac crests, must all be subtly but strongly rendered
if life and movement are to be achieved. As before stated the whole of this
mass is more or less convex. The back of the figure is marked by the central
depression occupied by the vertebral column, the muscles being arranged symmetrically on either side. Here, again, the thorax forms an evenly balanced
mass, and though well covered by muscular sheets, is traceable in the general
contour.

Trapezius.—The upper part is covered by the trapezius, which arises from
the base of the skull, and the spines of the dorsal and cervical vertibræ, and is
attached to the spine of the scapula and outer third of the clavicle (Fig. 22).
The directions of the fibres should be observed and the clay laid on accordingly.
The twisting plane from the back of the neck over the shoulder to the clavicle
is full of vitality. The upper part of the muscle is marked by a diamond-shaped
depression in the centre of which lies the prominent spine of the 7th cervical.
The outer edge of the muscle tucks into the spine of the scapula, whilst the
lower portion is modified by the underlying shoulder-blade, which is more or
less visible according to the pose of the arm. In the space between the trapezius
and the latissimus dorsi lies a group of muscles which animates the shoulder-
blade. The lower part of the back is covered by the latissimus, wrapping itself
round the thorax and passing down to its attachments at the lumbar and sacral
spines, and the posterior third of the iliac crest (Fig. 22). On either side of the
vertebral spines are the erectore spinæ muscles, enriching the depression caused
by the supra spinous ligament, into which, on either side, the latissimus merges
in a curved line. The posterior iliac spines have already been noted, and above
these the back is completed by the external oblique which stretches from the
ribs to the iliac crest. Below lie the gluteus maximus and the gluteus medius
swelling out into the full rounded forms of the buttocks, with a deep depression
at the sacrum and coccyx, and a flattened plane on the outer side which is caused
by the ileo tibial band (Fig. 25). Here, again, the directions of the fibres should
be observed in the modelling or the buttocks will be shapeless lumps instead of
interesting muscular forms. The crease between the buttocks demands attention, its direction should be noted, together with the contraction of the
fibres on the side of the standing leg, and the relaxation and elongation on the
side of the free leg. Note carefully the difference between the two sides, for
only by a truthful rendering can the movement here be suggested (Figs. 11 and
23). Get your drawing correct at the crease and beneath the buttocks, for
no part, however unimportant it may seem, can be scamped without losing some
essential quality in the figure. The back of the figure is, like the front, full of
beautiful forms, which need concentration and careful study if they are to be
represented with anything like truth.

Triceps of Thigh.—The front of the thigh depends largely upon the
triceps, *i.e.* the rectus femoris, the vastus internus and the vastus externus,
attached above to the ilium and femur and below by a common tendon to the
patella. On the outer side the triceps are bounded by the tensor fasciæ
femoris, and the ileo tibial band, which accounts for the flattened plane on the
outer side of the thigh. Inside the boundary is formed by the sartorius, a long
band-like muscle sweeping round from the anterior iliac spine to the inner side
of the shaft of the tibia (Figs. 19 and 25). The muscular forms are well defined
and the difference between fibre and tendon plainly visible, so that anatomical

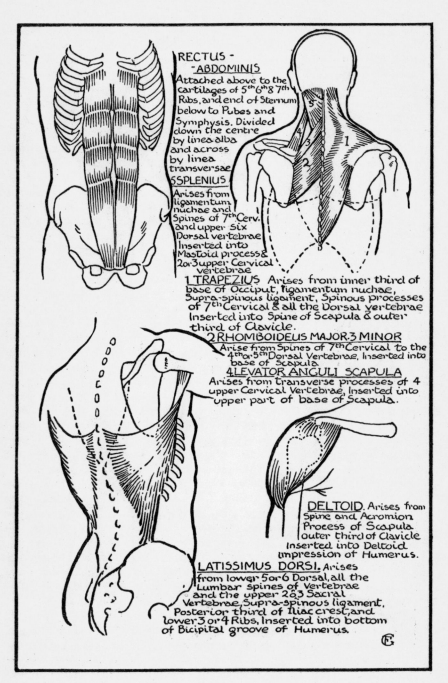

RECTUS -
-ABDOMINIS
Attached above to the
cartilages of 5th 6th & 7th
Ribs, and end of Sternum
below to Pubes and
Symphysis. Divided
down the centre
by linea alba
and across
by linea
transversae
5 SPLENIUS
Arises from
ligamentum
nuchae and
Spines of 7th Cerv.
and upper Six
Dorsal vertebrae
Inserted into
Mastoid process &
2 or 3 upper Cervical
vertebrae
1 TRAPEZIUS Arises from inner third of
base of Occiput, ligamentum nuchae,
Supra-spinous ligament, Spinous processes
of 7th Cervical & all the Dorsal vertebrae
Inserted into Spine of Scapula & outer
third of Clavicle.
2 RHOMBOIDEUS MAJOR. 3 MINOR
Arise from Spines of 7th Cervical to the
4th or 5th Dorsal Vertebrae, Inserted into
base of Scapula
4 LEVATOR ANGULI SCAPULA
Arises from transverse processes of 4
upper Cervical Vertebrae, Inserted into
upper part of base of Scapula.

DELTOID. Arises from
Spine and Acromion
Process of Scapula
outer third of Clavicle
Inserted into Deltoid
impression of Humerus.
LATISSIMUS DORSI. Arises
from lower 5 or 6 Dorsal, all the
Lumbar spines of Vertebrae
and the upper 2 & 3 Sacral
Vertebrae, Supra-spinous ligament,
Posterior third of Iliac crest, and
lower 3 or 4 Ribs, Inserted into bottom
of Bicipital groove of Humerus.

FIG. 22.—Trunk and Shoulder Muscles.

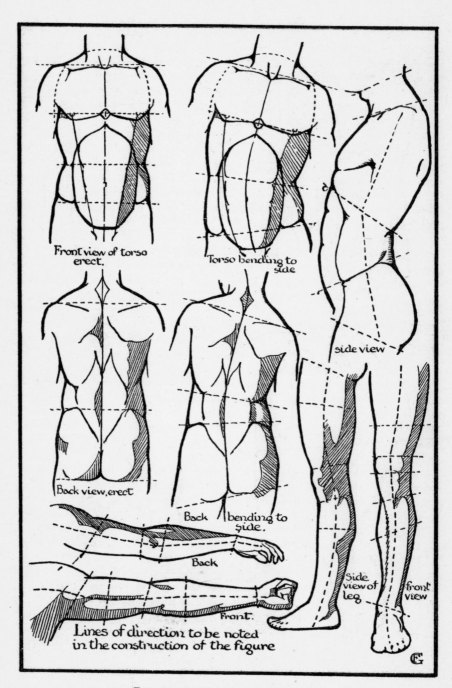

FIG. 23.—Construction of the Figure.

knowledge in building up the forms is indispensable. Just above the patella of the standing leg, a fullness may be noted which cannot be accounted for by muscle, bone, or tendon. This is caused by the synovial gland, which lubricates the knee joint. On the bent leg it has no effect upon the surface forms, leaving the common tendon of the triceps and the patella as the determinants of the forms. The group of muscles lying on the upper, inner border of the thigh, between the sartorius and the pelvis, are compact and affect the surface as a mass rather than as separate muscles (Fig. 25). Note the contraction of the muscles on the standing leg, in contrast with the loose, relaxed ones on the bent leg. Get a clear grasp of the planes, and the section of the thigh, which is by no means cylindrical. The difference between muscle and tendon must be suggested, whilst the hard, bony form of the patella gives a sharp note at the knee. The back of the thigh swells out from beneath the buttocks in well-defined planes, becoming tendinous and thinner above the knee, with a slight depression in the centre (Figs. 19 and 25).

Leg Muscles.—The leg below the knee is marked in front by the curved plane of the tibia, hard and bony, modified slightly by the tibialis anticus. The gastrocnemius and soleus take up the contour on the inner side, and also to some extent on the outer (Figs. 20-24). The group which lies between the tibialis and the soleus on the outer side form an interesting plane, broken somewhat by the fibres and tendons of the muscles. The ankle bones projecting from the slender shape above lead the lines outwards and so down through the foot to the ground. The greatest projection of the calf on the outer side is higher than on the inner, whilst the external malleolus is lower than the internal, two lines of contrast being thus afforded in the leg (Fig. 24). The back of the leg is notable for the swelling of the gastrocnemius above, and of the soleus on either side of the flat tendon Achilles by means of which they are attached to the os calcis (Fig. 24). There is exquisite form in the leg, making it well worthy of careful analysis. It is composed of flat planes, and rich, swelling muscular shapes, contrasting with hard bony surfaces. The foot needs careful treatment. The arch must be realised and also the line of contact with the ground. The grouping of the toes, and the wider space between the great toe and the first must be noted. The foot should seem to grip the ground, and not melt indeterminately into it. Too much care cannot be expended upon this line of contact between the foot and the base, as the eye travelling down the figure and reaching the base should at once feel that the whole is well poised, and yet firmly planted, an impression that is either emphasised or diminished by the drawing of this line.

The Deltoid.—The arm is crowned by the deltoid, a triangular muscle, arising from the outer parts of the clavicle and the spine of the scapula and inserted into the deltoid impression on the shaft of the humerus. The radiation of its fibres gives considerable movement to the planes in this region (Fig. 22). On the front of the arm the biceps muscle swells out below the deltoid and tucks in again at its lower end to a tendon which is attached to the tuberosity of the radius. The fibres are now inserted into this tendon, in a line at right angles to the arm, but one inclined downwards and inwards towards the body (Figs. 26 and 27). The triceps at the back form a similar line, inclined downwards and inwards. There is here a strong contrast between the muscle and the wide, flat tendon by means of which the triceps is inserted into the olecranon process (Fig. 27).

The Forearm.—The forearm is composed of two main groups of muscles,

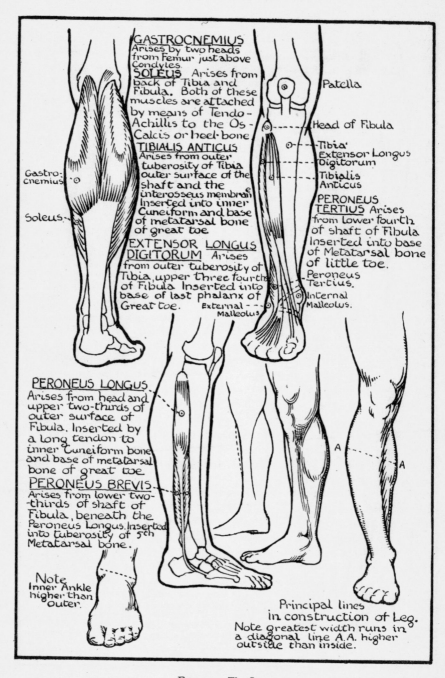

GASTROCNEMIUS Arises by two heads from Femur just above Condyles.

SOLEUS Arises from back of Tibia and Fibula. Both of these muscles are attached by means of Tendo-Achillis to the Os-Calcis or heel·bone

TIBIALIS ANTICUS Arises from outer tuberosity of Tibia Outer surface of the shaft and the interosseus membran Inserted into inner Cuneiform and base of metatarsal bone of great toe.

EXTENSOR LONGUS DIGITORUM Arises from outer tuberosity of Tibia, upper three fourths of Fibula Inserted into base of last phalanx of Great toe.

Gastro-cnemius

Soleus

External Malleolus

Patella

Head of Fibula

Tibia·
Extensor Longus Digitorum
Tibialis Anticus

PERONEUS TERTIUS Arises from lower fourth of shaft of Fibula Inserted into base of Metatarsal bone of little toe.

Peroneus Tertius.

Internal Malleolus.

PERONEUS LONGUS Arises from head and upper two-thirds of outer surface of Fibula. Inserted by a long tendon to inner Cuneiform bone and base of metatarsal bone of great toe

PERONEUS BREVIS Arises from lower two-thirds of shaft of Fibula, beneath the Peroneus Longus. Inserted into tuberosity of 5th Metatarsal bone.

Note Inner Ankle higher·than Outer.

A

A

Principal lines in construction of Leg. Note greatest width runs in a diagonal line A.A. higher outside than inside.

FIG. 24.—The Leg.

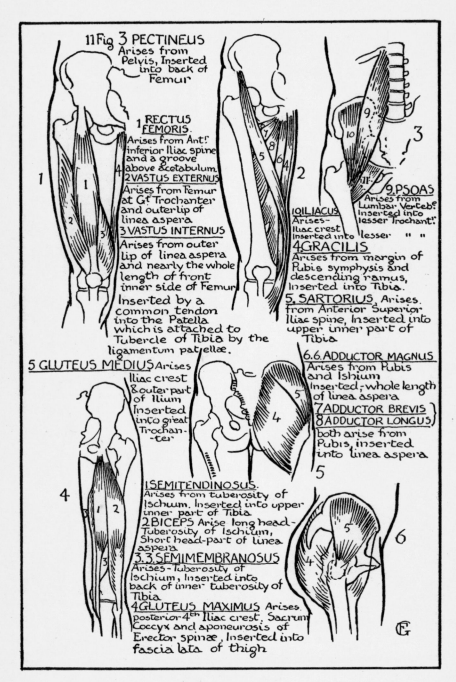

11 Fig 3 PECTINEUS
Arises from
Pelvis, Inserted
into back of
Femur

1 RECTUS
FEMORIS.
Arises from Ant!
inferior Iliac spine
and a groove
above acetabulum.
2 VASTUS EXTERNUS
Arises from Femur
at Gt Trochanter
and outer lip of
linea aspera
3 VASTUS INTERNUS
Arises from outer
lip of linea aspera
and nearly the whole
length of front
inner side of Femur
Inserted by a
common tendon
into the Patella
which is attached to
Tubercle of Tibia by the
ligamentum patellæ.

10 ILIACUS
Arises-
Iliac crest
Inserted into lesser

9. PSOAS
Arises from
Lumbar Verteb?
Inserted into
lesser Trochant!
lesser " "

4 GRACILIS
Arises from margin of
Pubis symphysis and
descending ramus,
Inserted into Tibia.

5. SARTORIUS. Arises
from Anterior Superior
Iliac spine, Inserted into
upper inner part of
Tibia

5 GLUTEUS MEDIUS Arises
Iliac crest
& outer part
of Ilium
Inserted
into great
Trochan-
-ter

6.6. ADDUCTOR MAGNUS
Arises from Pubis
and Ishium
Inserted - whole length
of linea aspera
7 ADDUCTOR BREVIS
8 ADDUCTOR LONGUS
both arise from
Pubis, inserted
into linea aspera

1 SEMITENDINOSUS.
Arises from tuberosity of
Ischium, Inserted into upper
inner part of Tibia
2 BICEPS Arise long head-
Tuberosity of Ischium,
Short head-part of linea
aspera
3.3. SEMIMEMBRANOSUS
Arises-Tuberosity of
Ischium, Inserted into
back of inner tuberosity of
Tibia
4 GLUTEUS MAXIMUS Arises
posterior 4th Iliac crest. Sacrum
Coccyx and aponeurosis of
Erector spinæ, Inserted into
fascia lata of thigh

FIG. 25.—The Thigh.

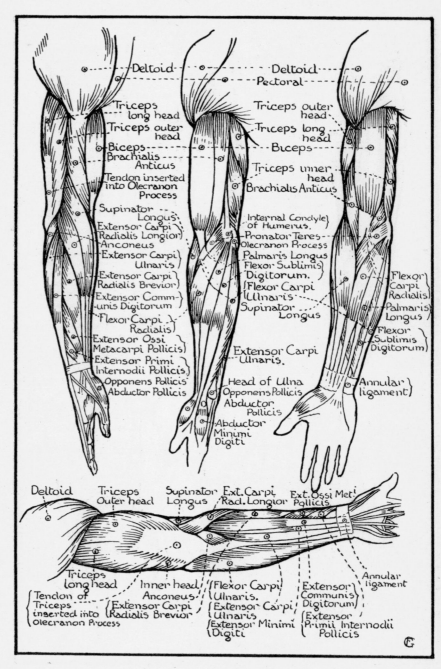

FIG. 26.—The Arm.

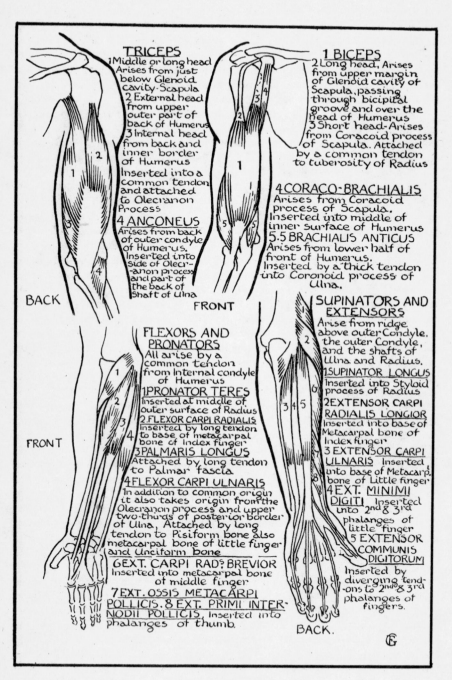

FIG. 27.—The Arm.

the flexors and pronators which arise from the internal condyle of the humerus, and the supinators and extensors arising from the external condyle and the shafts of the ulna and radius. These groups are fleshy and rounded above, becoming flattened and tendinous towards the wrist (Figs. 26 and 27). An opportunity is here afforded for representing the different qualities of fibre and tendon, and again of bone in the subcutaneous olecranon process and shaft of the ulna, and the heads of radius and ulna at the wrist.

The Hand.—The hand is full of character, and should not be neglected as is so often the case. Look for the curving lines at the knuckles and joints, note the movement carefully and do not treat them as details of no importance, for the hands give a finish to the figure and assist in the realisation of the pose. The head is of vital importance and must be well posed and constructed. Further analysis and suggestions for treatment are given in the section devoted to the modelling of the bust. The foregoing brief outline indicates the importance of anatomical construction in the modelling of the figure. It is of course unnecessary to detail each muscle with its fibres and tendons as would be the case if one were modelling an anatomical figure, but a construction that emanates from an intelligent application of anatomical knowledge will not only be more vigorous, but will proceed with less risk of failure and disappointment.

Value of Anatomy.—In building-up the figure a considerable amount of energy, both mental and physical, is required. It is necessary to be on the alert whilst engaged in the work ; any slackness or decrease in energy will be apparent in the modelling. It will become tired looking and flaccid. Lines of direction and contrast, alterations in planes and surfaces, must be carefully observed and rendered. The model should be observed from above and from below so that the sections of the various parts may be correct. Keep the whole of the work going together, bringing each part up to the same stage of development as the rest, or your work will lack homogeneity. Turn the model fairly frequently during the building-up stages, as by so doing you are prevented from working too long on one part, besides having the advantage of seeing the model and your work in different lights. Do not attempt to render the smooth texture of the surface until the whole has been analysed and built up anatomically. For this way lies disaster. You must dissect, peer into, and examine, get all the vitality you can into the clay before attempting to finish. It is so easy to smooth all the life out of the work when finishing, that it is safer to get all the life you can into it before commencing to finish. When, however, you are satisfied that you have got all you can into your figure, it is time to spread the skin over the muscles. This skin should be softer in consistency than that of which the underlying forms is composed, to enable you to spread a thin covering without displacing the forms below. Work this soft clay over and between the muscular and bony construction, blending and combining it without obliterating any essential form (Plate XI.). Note also the depressions that occur between the masses. You will find no sharp angles between the forms in the figure, but always a delicate bridging of the space which adds immeasurably to its breadth and suppleness. This bridging of the spaces between the forms requires much care and study, for if the hollow is too deep your work will look restless and cut up, whereas if the hollow is filled in too much it will become smooth and empty. But due emphasis given to these little planes that occur between the forms will add much to the refinement and elegance of the figure. A study of the section will help considerably in judging the depths of the hollows

PLATE XI.

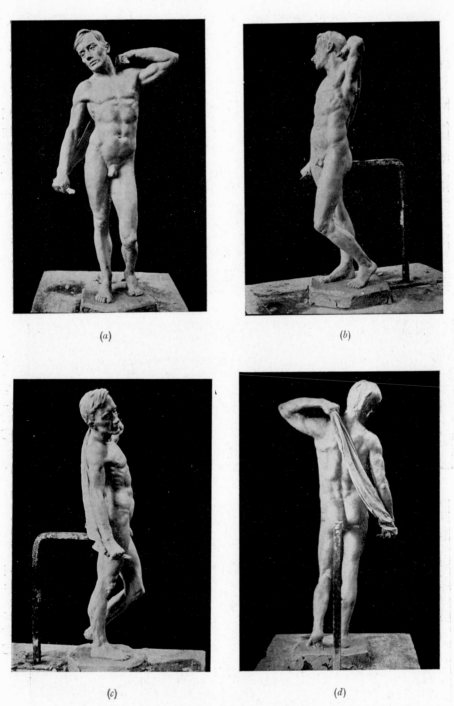

(a)   (b)

(c)   (d)

MODELLING THE FIGURE FROM LIFE.

PLATE XII.

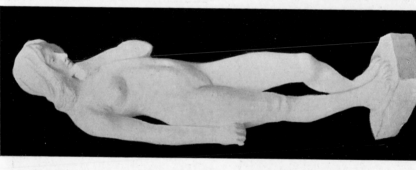

(a) By F. Shurrock.

(b) By the Author.

(c) By F. Shurrock.

STUDIES FROM LIFE.

(Figs. 28 and 29), or a straight-edge might be laid upon the projections at either side, and the depression judged from this. Keep the model and your work turning, so that the lighting changes, as by so doing you will see the forms under

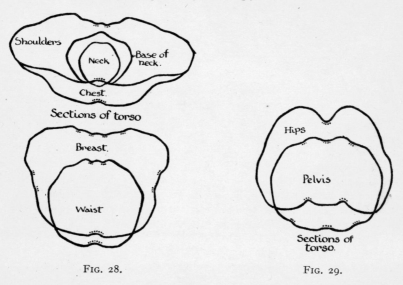

Sections of torso

FIG. 28.   FIG. 29.

different conditions, and will be able to render them with greater truth. In this last stage it is often advisable to work across the forms instead of continuing in the direction of bone, tendon, and fibre, as was advised when building-up.

Differences between Male and Female Figures.—The male figure has been chosen for purposes of demonstration, because the construction is more clearly exhibited and the forms more obvious than in the female figure. The greater thickness of the superficial fatty layer tend to soften the modelling, and to make the forms less apparent than in the male. When treating the female figure the characteristic differences between the sexes should be borne in mind. In the female the thorax is relatively smaller and the pelvis broader and shallower. The collar-bones are less horizontal and the bones generally slighter. The result of this is : the shoulders slope outwards and downwards more distinctly, the upper portion of the trunk is smaller, while the hips are wider than in the male. Another distinctive feature is the mammary glands or breasts. The angles at which these are set on the thorax should be carefully noted. Plate XII. (*a*), by Francis Shurrock, and Plate XII. (*b*), by the author, show two female figures. Plate XII. (*c*), a further example of Mr. Shurrock's work, illustrates the subtle modelling peculiar to a youthful figure.

CHAPTER V.

RELIEF WORK.

THERE are various types of relief treatment, though we are accustomed to grouping them all under two heads : Bas-relief and Alto-relief, which terms are used rather to indicate the type of work, than the projection of the modelling.

Bas-relief.—Bas-relief is the name applied to work in which the planes entering into it are but slightly differentiated in height from one another. The contour of the general mass may be raised considerably above the ground, but if the planes within the contour are but slightly relieved, no matter how much the work stands above the ground, the term bas-relief is employed.

Alto-relief.—An alto-relief is one in which the difference between plane and plane in the actual modelling is greater than in a bas-relief. In a portrait, for instance, profile, the plane of the nose may be almost coincident with the ground, but the cheek-bone, side of the head, brow, and ear will stand well above it, may, in fact, be almost as salient as in the model. Vasari differentiates between the various relief treatments more explicitly. He speaks of pictorial or perspective relief, where the principal figures in half-relief or more stand in front of those on the next plane, who again are in advance of those on the third plane. He condemns those artists who endeavour to produce effects of perspective, legitimate only in painting, for, he says, " They made their principal figures stand on the plane which is in low relief and recedes, and the middle figures on the same plane in such a position that, as they stand, they do not rest their feet firmly as is natural, whence it not unfrequently happens that the points of the feet of those figures that turn their backs, actually touch the shins of their own legs, so violent is the foreshortening . . . therefore, such reliefs of this character are incorrect." He truthfully points out, that the ancients used their figures correctly, placing them all with their feet resting on the moulding beneath them. He next deals with low reliefs (*bassi rilievi*) which project much less than the half-relief, and having not more than half the boldness of the others, may rightly be used to suggest pictorial effects, without danger of " errors or barbarisms." Last on his list comes flat reliefs (*stiacciati rilievi*), a low, flattened relief, demanding great skill in design and invention. " Donatello worked better here than did any other," says Vasari, and one is inclined to agree with him, for the delicate work produced in this manner by Donatello is really exquisite. Plate XXXIV. by Settignano, and Plate XXXVIII. of the school of Donatello are typical examples.

LOW RELIEF (BAS–RELIEF).

Low relief is one of the most difficult modes of plastic expression, and it is certainly one of the most fascinating. Subtlety and delicacy are indispensable, whilst good shapes and a well-schemed harmony of line and mass are absolute essentials. The student is advised to commence by making studies from the human figure, or from casts of hands, feet, limbs, and later a head, after which the full figure and compositions may be attempted. The problem for solution is the representation of projections of considerable height by means of a relief that is perhaps not more than half an inch at the highest points. This may be achieved by a skilful superposition of planes, each of which must be well drawn, and carefully thought out. A sharply-defined plane, lying above another equally well-defined, with others subtly indicated, will suggest a sense of relief sufficient for any purpose that comes within the legitimate scope of this method of treatment. The outline necessarily plays a very important part in the scheme, and generally a clear trenchant edge, particularly where the modelling is relieved against the background, is best. But to some extent this depends upon the effect we are aiming at, for by merging the edge with the ground, and by " losing and finding " it, a sense of distance may be obtained. Upon the treatment of this edge, much of the modelling depends. Forms that we wish to stand away from the ground, or from other forms that lie in a lower plane, should be strongly outlined. Distant forms may blend into the ground, so as to be faintly discernible, and so by a judicious rendering of edges, by a thoughtful insistence upon one part, and a careful modification of another, it is possible to produce work which shall have the appearance of considerable relief when its highest parts are but half an inch or even less.

Anatomy.—A knowledge of anatomy is quite as essential for relief work as for work in the round, the more so as forms are suggested rather than actually realised, and unless we are very decided about the make-up of the figure we can hardly hope to make the work convincing. It is therefore hardly advisable to attempt figure work in relief until a knowledge of construction has been acquired by modelling in the round. For it is much easier to copy forms, when we are permitted to model them similar in bulk to the original, than it is when we can only suggest by a subtle disposition of planes and surfaces. The callipers are practically useless here, for only such parts as lie in a plane parallel to the ground will appear their actual length, all other portions will be more or less foreshortened. Hence measuring is not to be recommended, any more than it would be in a drawing. It is better to rely upon one's sense of proportion, working freely and not hampering oneself with measurements.

Architectural Work.—Where the work is to be placed in an architectural setting, the projection, style, and method of treatment is determined by surroundings. A block of stone is left for us to ornament, and we must do this with due regard for position, lighting, and surrounding members. Our first studies will progress more confidently, however, if unhampered by any considerations other than the representation of the model. We will commence then with a cast of a hand, foot, or arm, whichever happens to be most convenient.

Clay Ground.—First prepare a ground of suitable size, by nailing four battens or strips of wood to a stout board, and after damping the enclosed space, fill it with moderately hard clay. Roll the clay between the hands and press the resulting pieces into position until the clay is level with the top of the strips. Level the surface with a straight-edge (Fig. 1) ; fill up any hollows that may be left, and level again. Do this until you have a perfectly smooth surface. Now, carefully consider the shape and size of the detail you are copying, and place it well on the ground, by sketching the contours lightly but firmly on the clay.

Get into the habit of placing your study well on the ground, regard each study as an exercise in space-filling as well as an exercise in relief modelling. This may seem unnecessary in a mere study, but it tends to make your future efforts at composition easier, and it certainly enhances the value of the work if the background shapes are pleasant, in addition to the raised portions. Treat everything you do as a whole, consider the entire panel rather than confine your attention to the detail you are engaged upon. Having sketched the contours of your study upon the background the next stage is to raise the forms. There are two ways of doing this. One is to cut away the ground with a suitable wire tool, leaving your study as a raised flat plane, which is then worked into

FIG. 30.—Planes of the Head.

FIG. 31.—Planes of the Hand.

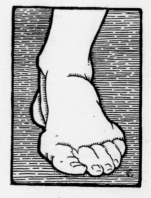

FIG. 32.—Planes of the Foot.

shape. The other is to gradually build up by adding the necessary clay. The first method is useful in some cases, but the latter is preferable for most relief work. Cutting away the ground makes it a difficult matter to keep that ground

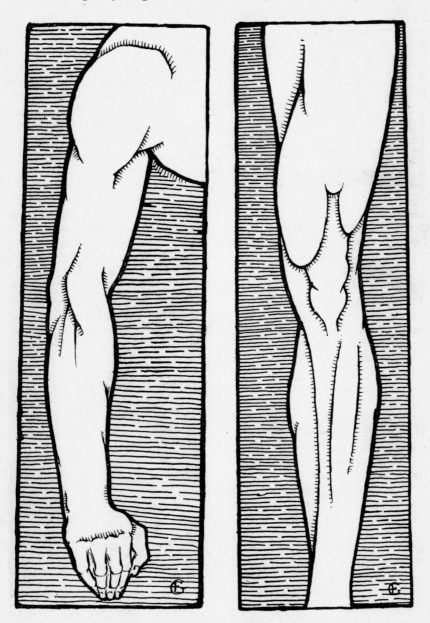

FIG. 33.—Planes of the Arm and Leg.

level, and an uneven surface makes a subtle treatment of edges much harder. Besides which the carving of the forms from the raised surface is somewhat alien to the spirit of modelling, which consists of adding the necessary forms rather than cutting away till you arrive at them.   It is better in most cases, therefore, to build up, leaving the level surface of the ground untouched.

Building-up.—It is here that the whole difficulty of the method comes in,

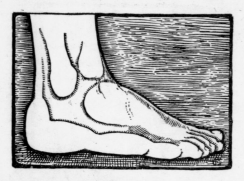

for now we must decide upon the relative heights of the various planes, their shapes, sizes, and directions.   Get your work into a strong side light, which should be varied from time to time as the work proceeds.   The drawings (Figs. 30-35) may serve to indicate the relationship of the planes in the various parts, but only in a rough diagrammatic way.   In the head (Fig. 30), for instance, the ear will project slightly beyond the planes of the cheek and hair.

Fig. 34.—Planes of the Foot.

The cheek and brow are higher than the eye, below which again come the nose and mouth, with other planes sloping between, subtly blending them together. The line of the jaw is above the neck and throat, with the sterno mastoid slightly

in advance of the other parts of the neck.   In the torso (Fig. 35) the pectorals form planes higher than the sternum, the mass of ribs, and the serrati.   The rectus abdominis forms a series of subtly rounded planes, raised above the surrounding aponeurosis, and so on.   But any amount of description is not half so valuable as a careful look at the model or cast. The student must learn to see these planes for himself, and must make up his mind definitely about the shapes of them.   It is fatal to attempt to model a form of which you have but a vague, indefinite idea ; each form must be analysed and thoroughly grasped before it is attempted in clay.   You cannot hope to flick the clay about and get what you require by a happy accident — things don't happen that way in modelling.   The only way to learn is to search every surface and find out exactly how

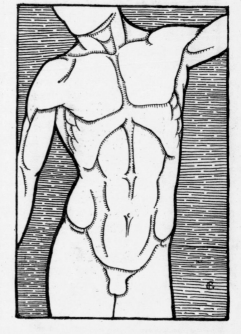

Fig. 35.—Planes of the Trunk.

it is made up, after which comes the further labour of reproduction.   The first stage of a relief should be vigorous (Plate XIII. (*a*), (*b*)), with every form well defined, in fact a series of definitely shaped planes.   After this comes the finishing, and here again, as in work in the round, it is astonishingly easy to lose all the vitality possessed by the earlier, more trenchant stage.

Finishing.—The final skin should be of clay rather softer than that of which the underlying forms is composed. It should be possible to spread a thin layer of this soft clay over the work without disturbing the planes beneath, so that the whole may be blended and brought together into one homogeneous whole. The spaces or hollows that lie between the projections are vitally important. There must be a breadth of surface between the forms rather than a sharp crevice, for nothing looks meaner in sculpture than a thin, scratchy hollow. This applies to all work, whether in the round or in relief, but if it is true of work in the round, where actual projections and hollows of correct depth may be copied, it is much more so in low relief, where breadth of surface and stern restraint are necessary, if we do not wish the result to appear fussy, restless, and unsatisfying. A little practice is necessary before one can spread the soft clay over and between the forms, but if the clay is right, and the thumb and fingers are kept damp by means of a wet sponge, it can soon be learned. Plate XIII. (*a*), (*b*) indicates two stages in the building-up of a portrait study, whilst Plate XIII. (*c*), (*d*) shows examples of finished studies. Note the strength of the forms in the masculine head (Plate XIII. (*d*)) as compared with the more subtle modelling in the feminine head (Plate XIII. (*c*)). Plate XIII. (*e*) is a relief study of an arm. The modelling is nowhere more than three-eighths of an inch above the ground, but being strongly lit from above, appears more.

A PORTRAIT STUDY IN RELIEF.

After a little practice it is an excellent plan to attempt a portrait study. It is usually possible to get a friend to sit for you, but, failing this, it is quite easy to be one's own model, by using a couple of mirrors, assuming that you wish to try a profile. One is placed parallel to the side of the head and the other in front, so that the image from the side mirror is reflected into the one in front, becoming visible each time you look up from your work. It is hardly necessary to state that a profile is much easier, and on the whole, I think, more satisfactory in low relief than a full face or even a three-quarter. When you have settled on your model, or arranged the mirrors, as the case may be, it is advisable to make a careful drawing and to arrange on paper the pose of the head and its position in the panel. The background is then prepared and the contours outlined with a suitable modelling tool. The next stage is to build up the forms, taking care to keep the whole within the limits decided upon, for it seems irresistible at first to keep piling on the clay in a vain endeavour to get the appearance of the head by means of sheer bulk. Search out the planes, and realise them in clay, keeping the whole trenchant and decided (Plate XIII.). A wire tool is very useful for getting the flat surfaces, and the student should endeavour to resolve the whole head into a series of flat planes, definite in shape and right in direction. These planes may be softened and rounded later if necessary, but should be kept square and decided at first. Note carefully the character of your model, for it is a portrait you are attempting; render the various forms with fidelity and pay particular attention to the pose of the head. Note the model's usual manner of carrying his head, for in this is expressed a considerable amount of character. If the head is held high it suggests a confident outlook; a drooping head may mean thought and a reflective tendency, or despondency. If posed sideways it may suggest a quizzical, humorous temperament, or perhaps an exaggerated humility as in Uriah Heep.

Placing the Head in the Panel.—There is distinct character in the pose of the head. Again, place the head well in the panel, with rather more space in front than behind, for a head cannot look well when the nose seems likely to come into contact with the margin. The head being well placed in the panel with varied spaces between it and the margins, and the forms carefully considered and blocked in, it is time to pull the modelling together. Don't be afraid to give a slight emphasis to the essential forms. These we have learnt something of from our work in the round, from study of the features and the skull. It is by no means a bad plan to " let the bones show." This pulling together or spreading of a thin, soft film of clay over the underlying structure is equivalent to adding a skin. It requires considerable care to veil, without obliterating, the essential forms, but as previously stated keep the thumb and fingers moist, and use softer clay than that of which the rest is composed. Watch carefully the spaces that occur between the projections, and avoid anything resembling scratches. It is possible after a little practice to suggest the textures of bone, flesh, cartilage, and hair, thereby adding interest and vitality to the work.

Hair Treatment.—The hair presents considerable difficulty, but by studying the masses, and the directions of the planes formed by the masses it is possible to get a sculpturesque and truthful rendering (Plate XIII. (*c*), (*d*)). It is, of course, hopeless to attempt the individual hairs, and to streak the head over with incised lines is to lose sight of the big masses, and will only lead to a worried, archaic effect. Here, again, there is a good deal of character. Some heads will have crisp curls, others a sweeping wave, others, again, straight lank hair, and some will have but little, merely a few strands tenderly pulled across a shining dome from which it has almost departed. The character of the hair must be seized and faithfully represented, its planes well considered, and the edges of the masses broken up to suggest the texture. In fact, it is in these edges that the bulk of the suggestion of texture lies. Again, dark hair requires a more trenchant treatment than fair hair. The deeper shadows serve to convey the impression of darker colour. But all these refinements are best learned by studying good examples ; it is only possible here to suggest what to look for, the rest depends on the student. It is only by earnest study that good work is produced, and there is no royal road to excellence. Study and constant practice are the only means whereby a good technique can be acquired.

Plaster Mould.—When you have carried the study as far as your are able in the clay, a plaster mould should be made. Build a wall around your panel, by laying strips of clay or wood from 1½ inches to 2 inches high by 1 inch thick in contact with the board. Leave a space of about 1 inch between the wall and the edge of the panel, which will give you a framed hollow into which to pour the plaster for your final cast, after the mould is made. If preferred, the wall may be placed in close contact with the edge, in which case it will be necessary to construct a wall around the mould before pouring in the plaster for your cast. When the wall is in position, gauge the amount of water required, into which the plaster is allowed to fall by letting it trickle between the fingers, until you see it appear evenly just below the surface. Allow a few seconds for the plaster to soak, and then stir vigorously until a smooth even mixture of the consistency of thick cream is obtained. Pour over the clay, shaking to exclude the air. Pour off again, leaving a thin film of plaster over the whole surface. If any hollows are not filled, or if any air bubbles have prevented the plaster from covering any portion, it is quite easy to blow the plaster over or into the parts not covered. Pour the plaster back over the panel and allow half an hour or so for it to set. When thoroughly hard, it may be lifted by inserting a broad knife between it and the board, pouring water over at short intervals. Wash the surface of the mould, and clean off any clay that may adhere ; when it is ready for working upon.

Work in the Mould.—A good deal of fine detail may be added by working in the mould, either with steel plaster tools, or with the boxwood modelling tools. Remember that your work is now reversed, and that any hollow or line incised in the plaster will appear as a projection on the final cast. Little touches may be given to the hair, beard, moustache, or other parts where a sharp projection is valuable. If lettering is introduced, it is a good plan to incise it in the mould, after having drawn the inscription on the clay before making the mould. For the lettering is now in reverse and unless you have drawn and spaced the characters beforehand, it is not so simple a matter doing it in the mould. If there are any sharp hollows or deep, scratchy lines that you wish to get rid of, they can be softened by wiping with a linen rag. A pitted or uneven surface can be made smooth by scraping off the excrescences by which they are represented in the mould. The progress of your work at this stage may be watched by squeezing some soft clay into the mould where you have been busy. This shows the modelling as it will appear in the final cast, and enables you to judge of its effect.

Final Cast.—When you have done all you wish to the mould, swill it over with soda water, or brush over with soft soap (as described in section on Casting), and taking care that it is well saturated with water, pour in the plaster for your cast. When hard, pull the two apart and, if necessary, work over the surface again, after which another mould may be taken, and more work added, and another cast made. Usually it is unnecessary to make more than two moulds ; it is quite possible to get all you require out of these, but the process may be extended as far as you wish. When thoroughly dry the portrait study may be treated with shellac, wax, or in imitation of bronze.

CHAPTER VI.

DRAPERY.

WHEN planning a figure composition it is rarely possible to dispense with drapery. The pliant curvature of the folds and the freedom permissible in handling the material make it invaluable for bridging awkward gaps, for connecting lines otherwise separate, and for blending masses that, undraped, would be difficult to harmonise. There are laws of construction in drapery which must be as strictly observed as the anatomical laws governing the human figure. It is therefore advisable to make studies of drapery alone before attempting to use it on the figure, or for an important work.

Different Materials.—The nature of the fold is practically the same in all materials, though a heavy one, as flannel, will be richer and broader in its folds than a light material like muslin or linen. Again, a stiff substance like silk or satin will be sharper and more angular in fold than a soft one such as velvet. Despite these differences dependent upon the quality of the stuff, however, the character of the fold is fundamentally the same. It is easier to grasp this character in a fairly heavy material than in a lighter one as the forms are bolder and more decided. Flannel gives broad, rich folds and is hence a good material for first studies. If we take a piece of flannel and suspend it from a point it will arrange itself into tapering folds as shown in No. 1, Fig. 36. By studying the section of the folds we shall find that there are no angles, but fairly full curves (see section at A B). The convex folds which project from the general mass are contrasted by alternate concave ones equally rich in section, whilst the two sets blend one into the other without corners or angles, but rather in full, soft, undulating curves. This fact should be carefully noted, for students are inclined to neglect the hollows between the convex pipes as of little importance, often making them sharp in section and mean in modelling, whereas the concave hollows should receive as much attention as the prominent folds, being just as important to the appearance of the work. Unless they are treated with the same generosity and richness as the outstanding portions, the result will be thin and meagre, lacking in breadth and character. A careful study, in clay, of a simple arrangement like No. 1, Fig. 36, will assist the student in realising the section of the folds. Note, too, how they taper; in No. 1a the folds are traced through to the point of suspension. This tapering gives an interesting radiation of line which is further characteristic of drapery and also of great value in composition. Having studied drapery when suspended from one point, take a somewhat larger piece and hang it from two points as in No. 3, Fig. 36. This produces an entirely different set of folds, where those on the one side will be contrasted by another set in the opposite direction on the other side. Contrast is added to radiation, the variety becomes intensified. The weight of the material causes it to droop between the two points of suspension with a

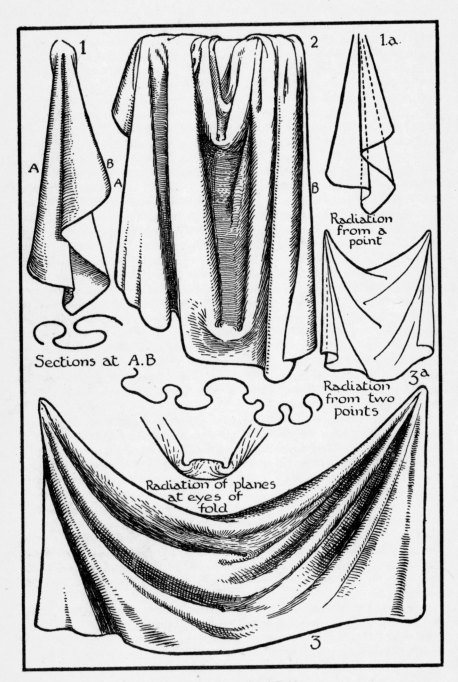

FIG. 36.—Analysis of Folds.

set of folds radiating on either side from these points. The folds are similar in section to those already dealt with, but where they meet in the centre further forms will be found for consideration. The general character of the arrangement is seen at No. 3a, where it will be noticed that in some cases the lines of the folds on one side continue beyond the actual centre before becoming merged into those on the other. In No. 2 a more generous use of the material, and a more vertical arrangement of the folds, produces rounder forms, and at the meeting points a series of loops or " eyes." There is less overlapping, the folds on one side do not extend into the other, but where it meets the opposing fold, forms an eye. These loops or eyes form interesting breaks, as they are full of vitality and subtlety. To get a clear idea of the fold here, take some clay and roll it between the hands until it assumes a slender cylindrical form. Lay the upper portion on a clay background, press the thumb into the cylinder near the centre and bend it at right angles. It will now be seen that the clay at this point has been forced outwards into greater prominence than the surrounding portions, whilst immediately within comes the depression forming the eye of the fold (see Fig. 36). Drapery loops itself in a similar manner and the eye is essentially the same in both. When studying the eye, observe carefully the play of the planes around the projecting point, how they radiate with an interesting variety of light and shade from the eye into the sweeping planes of the main folds. Unless these planes are observed and truthfully rendered the result will be flaccid and empty. These principles apply to drapery of all types though they will necessarily be modified or accentuated by the nature of the material in use. In soft, heavy stuffs, as velvet, the eye will naturally be rounder and less sharp than in silk, and bolder than in a lighter material like muslin. It is well to study the difference in quality dependent upon the nature of the drapery, as some works call for bold broad treatment, whilst others demand lighter, more revealing folds.

Study in Clay.—When the principles have been understood, the student should arrange a piece of flannel on a board as in Plate XIV. (*d*) and copy it in clay, for nothing will fix the knowledge in the mind like modelling. Care must be exercised to get an interesting set of varied folds. Now prepare a smooth background of clay, and arrange it conveniently, alongside the drapery, so that whilst working on the clay you can see the model without effort. Sketch in the main lines of the folds, selecting the most important; roll the modelling clay into slender cylindrical forms, and press them on the background to represent the folds, taking care to get them and the intervening spaces correct in proportion. Lay them in first from the front view, and then turn to the sides so that the projections may be studied and established. Note the positions of the eyes carefully, and copy the planes around them, giving these planes their due amount of play and movement.

Importance of Hollows.—As soon as the main folds are roughed in and the clay bears a skeleton resemblance to the drapery, turn your attention to the hollows, or concave surfaces. This is done for a double purpose, first, that these surfaces may be studied and accurately copied before they become partially hidden by the swelling convex folds, and second, that these convex projecting folds may not be knocked about when working the hollows as would be the case if the projecting folds were finished first. Further, by this plan, the hollows may be more successfully blended with the prominent folds and the planes swept continuously from one to the other with the result that the modelling

PLATE XIII.

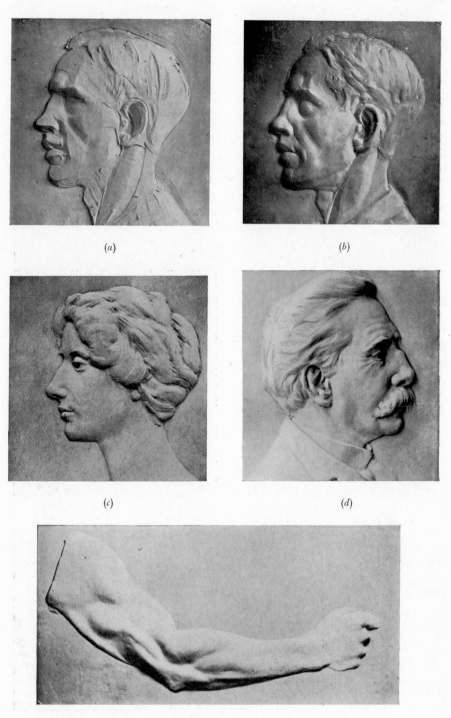

(a)

(b)

(c)

(d)

(e)

MODELLING IN LOW RELIEF.

PLATE XIV.

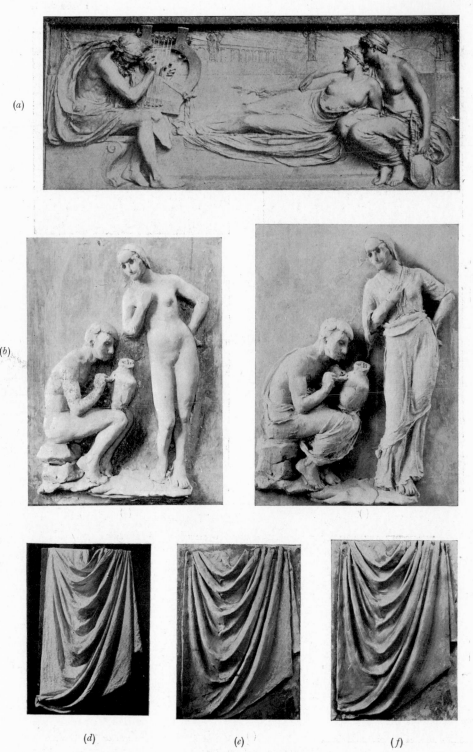

(a) RELIEF BY HARRY BATES. (b), (c) ROUGH CLAY FIGURES FOR DRAPING. (d) A HANGING DRAPERY. (e), (f) STAGES OF MODELLING DRAPERY SHOWN IN (d).

gains in breadth and truth (Plate XIV.).   It should be borne in mind that the hollows are similar in section to the projections, being similar folds reversed. Study the sections and this fact will be realised (Fig. 36, A, B and 2A, B).

Historic Study.—In conjunction with this study from the material, the work of the Greek, Gothic, Renaissance, and also modern sculptors, should be carefully examined.   Note the sections of the drapery, the manner in which it is arranged, and also how it is affected by the figure beneath.   When all the folds have been arranged, and are correct in projection and position, it is time to attend to the surface modelling.   A few wire tools and ball-ended boxwood ones are useful for finishing up the hollows, into which the fingers will not enter. A couple of fairly long hoghair brushes are valuable for smoothing these hollows, but they should be used with restraint, for it is only too easy to smooth all the character out of the work, leaving it smug and textureless.

Finish.—A fine finish full of character and expression can be given to the work by spreading soft clay over the folds.   This finishing clay should be considerably softer than that of which the underlying forms are composed, so that it may be spread thinly without disturbing the folds.   It must be applied with due regard for the direction of the planes and the texture of the material.   In some cases it will be advisable to work in the direction of the fold, and in other cases across it.   Upon the quality of the surface depends much of the character of the work.   At this stage the cloths used for keeping the clay damp should not be allowed to come into contact with the surface.   A few pegs of wood inserted at two or three projecting points, or a simple frame will serve to support the damp cloth and keep it away from the modelling.

The Draped Figure.—Having studied drapery arranged as described above, with a view to learning the character of the material and the section of the folds, the next stage is to study it when applied to the figure.   This is a much more difficult matter, as the lines of the material must be so disposed as to harmonise with those of the figure.   It is preferable in the majority of cases to arrange the drapery in such a way as to partly reveal and partly conceal the forms beneath.   The drapery should be moulded by the figure supporting it. A light, clinging stuff will naturally lie closer to the figure, leaving its forms more discernible.   Heavy materials, on the contrary, tend to veil the forms and to hang in broad, vertical folds, but unless the figure can be traced through the drapery, the work must inevitably lack interest and conviction.   The first study in this branch should be made from an arrangement of flannel or other fairly broad material, on a plaster cast.   By soaking the flannel in water and then wringing fairly dry it will lie in closer contact with the cast, giving greater prominence to its forms.

The Lay Figure.—In some cases where a particular pose is desired the lay figure will be found valuable, but as its resemblance to the human body is somewhat vague a good cast is always preferable.   Naturally the human figure is far more interesting, as every movement exhibits fresh arrangements, but owing to this very movement the folds are too changeable for translation into clay until such time as the student has acquired sufficient knowledge to work rapidly and confidently.   Much may be learned by watching the draped figure, and also by making studies in charcoal and chalk on a toned paper, in fact it is an excellent plan to make as many studies of this type as circumstances will allow, in conjunction with the modelled studies.   Having selected a cast, damp the flannel and lay it on the statue in such a way that the figure is revealed and at the same time the material falls into interesting folds.   The pose of the figure must be taken into consideration when arranging the folds in order that it may be emphasised by them instead of being concealed or antagonised.   The general trend of the principal mass of folds should contribute to the pose and action of the figure.   Variety must also be aimed at.   The principal fold or mass of folds should be contrasted with plain spaces, through which the underlying forms of the figure might be subtly revealed.   This variety will enhance the value of the folds and the spaces.   Further, where the folds are grouped they look better when varied.   Varied folds take a more interesting light and shade, and are altogether preferable to an even monotonous set.   When the drapery has been satisfactorily disposed it is time to commence modelling. The figure should first be built up on an armature as described in modelling the figure, not highly finished, but true in form on the more prominent surfaces, especially those which act as supports for the material.   The nude preparation should be fairly generous in modelling, as a slender figure becomes even more slender when draped.   The next stage in the work is to add the principal folds in the shape of long pipes or rolls of clay as we did when modelling the arrangement on the board.

Principal Folds.—The main ones are first placed in position with due regard for the pose of the figure and for harmony of line.   As the stuff has been already disposed on the cast with these principles in mind, it is better to copy as truthfully as possible.   Far more can be learned about drapery at this stage by careful copying of the folds before us, than by starting with a preconceived notion of what they should be and then striving to coerce them into the lines we wish them to take.   Later when a more thorough knowledge of the anatomy of drapery has been acquired, we may select and reject, amplify here and modify there, but our first studies should be conscientious renderings of the forms in the copy.   Note carefully how the material lies in close contact with the areas of support, falling away in a series of radiating folds as the supporting surface recedes, leaving the drapery hanging.   Sometimes these folds will fall vertically from the supporting areas, and sometimes they will be festooned between two prominent surfaces.   There is material here for much earnest study : the differences in the folds, the radiation of line, the variety between fold and plain area, the sections of the folds, and the modifications caused by underlying forms, and also by the nature of the drapery, will afford quite enough to keep the student absorbed whilst working at the draped figure.   Further studies should be made from casts draped with muslin, which, if damped, will cling to the forms in delicate revealing folds of great beauty and refinement.   Again, an under tunic of linen or light material might be varied by a cloak or mantle of flannel or other fairly heavy material thrown across.   The difference in the folds caused by the differing qualities of the material will add to the interest of the arrangement.   Figs. 37 and 38 indicate a few draped figures, whilst others will be found amongst the illustrations of historic work.   One of the most perfect examples of drapery on the human figure is " The Fates " (Plate XXVIII.).   Note how Phidias, in this beautiful work, has disposed his material in such a way as to emphasise the salient points in the figures.   Instead of concealing the forms, the light, clinging material lies in close contact with them on the areas of support, and elsewhere groups itself into sets of beautiful folds festooning between prominent portions, or winding around the limbs in a manner that serves to express only the more fully the exquisite contours beneath.   The delicate

FIG. 37.—Draped Figures.

FIG. 38.—Draped Figures.

variety of the folds where the drapery is full and voluminous forms a beautiful contrast to the simple surfaces moulded by the underlying limbs and torsos. Compare the treatment with that of Baccio Bandinelli in " Venus " (Plate XXXVII.), and it will at once be seen how far short the lesser man falls in his rendering. The terra-cotta relief ascribed to Donatello (Plate XXXVIII.) has much delicate suggestion in its modelling, though the child is somewhat stiffly enwrapped. A fine specimen of drapery in relief is the Sculptured Drum (Plate XXIX.), the arrangement of the folds being well worth studying.

A good plan when drapery is required for a composition is to rough up in high relief clay figures similar in pose to those in the design. These figures are then draped with muslin dipped in clay-water and wrung fairly dry (Plate XIV. (b), (c)). The damp material will lie in intimate contact with the forms, and when dry will retain the folds owing to the stiffening influence of the clay-water. This method is also excellent for studying the folds of flying drapery as the material can be fitted to the figure and the loose portions spread out upon the ground, flowing away from the figure in a manner similar to drapery blown by the wind. The advantage of working in this way will be at once appreciated if we watch some wind-blown drapery, or some upon a figure in rapid movement. The rapidity with which the folds change, and the fleeting forms taken by the material, make it an exceedingly difficult matter to choose even from the forms we are able to see. We can hardly make studies of drapery in motion unless we can fix some one of the many arrangements in our minds and work from memory. As an exercise this is excellent practice, but when it comes to working out the detail in a finished study we shall need to arrange our drapery on the clay figure, and the background as suggested. A further scheme for studying drapery in motion is to make a rough model in plaster or clay of a figure in the desired pose, and to drape it with muslin dipped in plaster. The figure is then supported on two trestles or handy supports in a horizontal position, the drapery being allowed to hang in the desired direction (generally behind the figure) and blown into such forms as are required with a pair of bellows. When the plaster has set, the figure can be placed in an upright position and the drapery will remain streaming out behind as though the wind were holding it. Vasari describes the method in vogue in his day for studying drapery, and it was very similar to ours. A figure was modelled in clay or wax and a fine, or heavy cloth (according to the desired result) dipped in clay-water and arranged round the figure in such folds or creases as the mind suggested. The " Maenad in Frenzy " (Plate XXVIII.) is a beautiful example of drapery in movement, while Plate XXXV., by Ghiberti, is full of suggestion.

CHAPTER VII.

COMPOSITION.

THE grouping of figures into a composition is one of the most difficult problems for the student of modelling as indeed it is for the student of any art, whether plastic or graphic. The human figure cannot be twisted and contorted into any pose or line that may be felt necessary for the desired result. The attitudes must be possible, and the lines graceful and easy. There must exist no feeling of strain, rather one of ease and natural movement, or the spectator will be assailed by an uncomfortable sensation that the figures are distorted and impossible. To achieve this, and at the same time to get a harmony of line and mass is by no means easy. In relief work the difficulties are not so great as they are in a composition in the round, for in a relief the work is viewed from one standpoint only, whereas in a group of statuary the lines and masses must be pleasing from every point of view.

Composition in the Round.—It is, therefore, of little value planning a group on paper which is to be modelled in the round, for on the flat, one aspect only out of the many can be dealt with. The group should, therefore, be planned directly in clay and studied from every side, or disappointment is bound to result. See that your lines and masses harmonise, that the group is well knit together with one line flowing into another and all leading to the culminating feature of the group. It is impossible to lay down definite rules for composition. It is so personal a matter, depending so largely upon the temperament, ability, and taste of the artist that any statements made about the disposition of line and mass are apt to appear dogmatic. It might truthfully be said that composition cannot be taught. It certainly cannot be reduced to rule-of-thumb methods, as this would inevitably lead to dead, uniform inanities. Rules cannot be formulated, composition is not so easy as this. The only guidance that can be offered is stated in a few sentences. See that all the lines in the group flow harmoniously into each other, and that the composition forms one complete whole. Legs and arms sticking out at awkward angles are apt to mar the *tout ensemble* of the group. They lead the eye out of the scheme, and unless it is returned by some other feature, it is left wandering aimlessly round the group, seeking some path of re-entry. Parallelism is another fault to be avoided. Radiation of line is invariably of greater interest than parallelism, hence the torsos and limbs of the figures entering into the scheme should rarely lie in parallel directions. Note the word rarely is used here, instead of never, for sometimes it is necessary to lay stress upon a certain line of direction which may be done by echoing it with a line parallel to it. This proves how difficult and dangerous it is to lay down hard and fast laws. But parallel lines certainly make for monotony, and radiating ones for variety.

You have only to note how universal is the principle of radiation in nature to realise its value in line arrangements. Rules are merely for guidance; when power has been acquired the artist obeys them or breaks them almost without thought of them, though at the back of his mind he is dimly conscious of their restraining influence. To the student this restraining influence is usually beneficial. A certain suavity of line is essential in a composition; an easy flow of line into line, of plane into plane, with a general trend towards the main feature of the group, is the only way to achieve that sense of completeness, of homogeneity, which a composition must possess. But here again it is possible to carry the rule too far, it may be that the lines have got too suave, that the effect is two gentle and graceful, lacking in strength; a contrast of some sort has become a necessity.

Contrast.—Musicians will often introduce a discord when the harmony becomes too sweet, and far from destroying the harmony it is emphasised by the difference. One realises the beauty of the arrangement by sheer contrast. It helps to restore a correct perception of values, which unbroken harmony, by its cloying sweetness, would tend to vitiate. The same principle is applicable to sculpture, to any art in fact; a sharp note of contrast will often restore the balance of a composition that threatened to become soft and sweet even to insipidity. Figures gracefully posed in smooth flowing lines may often be corrected by one rigidly upright, or by a severe vertical line of drapery, or architecture. Too many uprights often call for a horizontal. In fact, vertical and horizontal lines are invaluable as correctives, and for stabilising a composition; they should be emphatically introduced where necessary.

Light and Shade.—Another highly important factor in a composition is the light and shade. The balance of the darks against the lights, and the relative proportions of one to the other plays a large part in the ultimate effect. But as to the quantities of each, and how they shall be distributed, there is no law, can be none, in fact. The only advice is, get variety. Keep the lights and darks as varied in mass and shape as possible. Avoid equality as far as you can, consistently with good modelling and strength of grouping.

Drapery.—A thoughtful introduction of drapery is often of great service here. It may be used to enlarge one of two equal masses, or even to blend them into one large mass if the work requires it. It will probably be contended that all this does not help in the least when planning a group, that most of the advice consists of " don'ts." Which merely proves my previous statement that composition can hardly be taught. In a book, at any rate, it is most difficult, for one has to deal broadly with the subject. When dealing with the student individually, the instructor can detect and correct such tendencies as are likely to lead astray. He can assist in the development of the student's qualities, and lead him to a confident expression of his own personality. In a book it is impossible to do more than generalise, and to point out a few broad principles. The student is constrained to learn composition for himself, and doubtless this is the best and safest method. There is less danger of being swamped by the dominating personality of the master (should he possess one). Study the works of the masters, analyse them, endeavour to find out what it is that makes them great and noble, and then apply the knowledge so obtained to your own work. There is enough great sculpture in existence to suit all tastes. The severity of the Greek, the naturalism of Donatello and his followers, and the titanic vigour of Michelangelo will provide ample material for the formation of a style, whilst the works of Rodin, Alfred Stevens, Alfred Gilbert and many of the modern men should not be neglected. As we learn the lesson taught by the great ones of the past, it is wise to study the application of those lessons by the best men of to-day. Art is the expression of the thought of its own period, hence the work of to-day exhibits the trend of modern ideas. But, whilst studying the works of others, and learning what they have to teach, beware lest you sink your own personality : let your work be individual and expressive of yourself, for copying is not merely feeble but fatal. Plate XV. (a) is a composition in the round by Francis Shurrock, where the pyramidal arrangement of the three figures helps to build up the group and to lead the eye up to the principal central figure. There is a feeling of harmony between the architectural lines and the full, rich forms of the figures. The light and shade is also well managed, the sense of tragedy being emphasised by the veiled head of the symbolic figure. Plate XV. (b) is a single figure used as an adornment of architecture by Francis Shurrock. It is reminiscent of Michelangelo, and shows the value of studying the work of this master. Plate XIV. (a) is a beautiful relief by Harry Bates. The linking up of the figures by the lines in the drapery and the distant building is masterly, whilst the modelling and treatment of form shows skill and refinement.

PLATE XV.

(a)

(b)

COMPOSITIONS IN THE ROUND BY F. SHURROCK.

CHAPTER VIII.

PLASTER CASTING. WASTE MOULDS.

As modelling clay will shrink and crack unless baked or kept moist, work executed in it is usually converted into plaster. Casting in plaster is a ready means of turning the modelling into more permanent material, and the student should learn to cast his own work as soon as possible, for even though the ultimate material is bronze or marble, before the clay can be converted into either of these, a plaster cast is necessary. A panel is more easily cast than a work in the round, and is therefore better for a beginning.

Materials.—The materials necessary are: Two bowls (enamelled iron are best as they stand a lot of knocking about). One of these should be fairly large, for mixing a sufficient quantity of plaster, and the other a smaller one, more easily handled, for pouring the plaster. A large iron spoon, a mallet and a couple of blunt chisels. Some lengths of iron bar, half-inch square. A few steel plaster tools, a sponge, a large knife, and a couple of large hog-hair brushes are needed.

Colouring Matter.—For the first coating of plaster some colouring matter is necessary. Yellow ochre, raw sienna, or any earth colour should be used in preference to Prussian blue, crimson lake, or any colour with a tendency to stain. A blue bag (common washing blue) serves the purpose. Some common washing soda to prevent the mould from adhering to the cast. Soft soap and olive or sweet oil are also used for this purpose, but take longer to prepare, and owing to the lack of affinity between oil and water are more liable to air-bubbles. I have used nothing but soda-water for a number of years and much prefer it to the more tedious soap and oil. Before commencing it is well to have all materials at hand. The colouring matter should be placed in a vessel and sufficient water added to dissolve the powder. The soda (a large handful) dissolved in boiling water and then poured into a bucketful of cold. Take care that your soda-water is not too strong as it eats into the plaster; the above proportion is sufficient. If the soap and oil preparation is preferred, a spoonful (table) of soap is dissolved by stirring into a saucepan full of boiling water.

Procedure.—Having prepared your materials lay the panel flat upon a table and erect a wall of clay about it, an inch or so from the panel, first smearing with soft clay the board between the clay wall and the panel. This keeps the mould from sticking to the board. The clay wall is made by beating out a slab of clay rather less than an inch in thickness, and cutting it into strips of from 1 to 2 inches wide according to the size and height of relief of the panel. Build the clay wall so that it frames the modelling, pressing the clay edgewise on to the board, and blending well together at the angles. Take the large bowl and carefully gauge the amount of water required for a thin coating of plaster. Into this water pour some of the liquid colouring matter, avoiding the sediment. Or steep the blue bag in the water until it assumes a distinct blue tint. The reason for this colour will be apparent when the chipping stage is reached. Into the coloured water sprinkle the plaster by allowing it to trickle through the fingers, any hard lumps that may be in the plaster can thus be easily detected and thrown aside, besides which it loosens the powder and allows the water to percolate freely. When the plaster begins to appear evenly just below the surface of the water, enough has been sprinkled in. Allow a second or two for the water to soak through, then thrust the iron spoon down to the bottom of the bowl and stir briskly from side to side, keeping the spoon well down until the plaster is of the consistency of thick cream. The hand is preferable for stirring as any lumps can be readily detected and broken up, or, if hard, thrown aside. Don't be in too great a hurry to stir ; allow the plaster time to get saturated and lumps will be less liable to form.

Applying the Plaster.—This mixture is thrown on to the clay with the fingers, so as to form an even coating of rather less than a quarter of an inch in thickness. See that all the interstices are filled ; it is useful sometimes to blow the plaster into the hollows, and the board upon which the modelling rests should be tapped smartly to exclude air-bubbles. Having poured the plaster over the clay, pour it back into the bowl again, and again on to the clay, until it begins to set. This helps to ensure the covering of the whole work and the exclusion of air-bubbles. When this first coloured coating has set it must be brushed over with clay water, to prevent the outer thicker coating from sticking too tightly. Now mix a much larger quantity of plaster in clean uncoloured water, and pour over the coloured one. If the panel is of any size a few lengths of iron bar should be embedded in the plaster whilst soft, to keep the mould from warping.

Removing the Mould.—When the plaster has set (a matter of from ten to fifteen minutes should be allowed for this), the whole is placed in the sink and saturated with water. This does not affect the plaster when set, but softens and expands the clay, facilitating the separation. Remove the outer walls of clay, and insert the knife between the mould and the board, sliding it the whole way round, gently prising the mould upwards. Keep on pouring water between the two until you can lift the mould away from the board. Remove all the clay, thoroughly wash the surface of the mould with the sponge or brush, until all traces of clay have been removed. Sponge over with soda-water, swill again with clean water, and the mould is ready for the final cast. If, however, it is desired to use the soft soap and oil, the soap in a liquid condition is poured into the mould and allowed to soak in for a few minutes. Pour it off again, and sponge away any that remains. Allow a few more minutes for this to penetrate, then pour a few drops of olive or sweet oil into the palm of the left hand, and moisten the end of a clean brush with the oil. Brush over the surface of the mould until it has a diffused sheen, soak again in water and it is ready. Mix sufficient plaster with clean water, and pour into the mould, shaking and blowing where necessary, to exclude the air and to ensure covering the whole surface. Tilt the mould once or twice and allow the plaster to run over the surface, also pour it back and fore between mould and bowl a few times. It is a good plan to saturate some coarse wide-meshed canvas or tow in the plaster, and just before it sets spread it over the back of the cast, but don't allow it to appear on the surface. When thoroughly set, allowing from twenty minutes to half an hour for this purpose, place a sack or some soft material on the table, and lay the whole upon this, face downwards. The sack or other material is to ease the jarring resulting from the chipping which otherwise might crack the cast.

Chipping the Mould.—You now proceed to chip away the white portion of the waste mould. First chip around the irons and pull them away, the method of chipping afterwards will depend largely upon the nature of the relief. If fairly low, with no outstanding bosses, the chisel may be inserted between the white and coloured plasters, and the strengthener lifted off in large pieces. Should there be projections, however, this is dangerous, as the leverage exercised by such large masses breaking away is apt to lift off the modelling as well. It is safer in this case to keep the chisel vertical when chipping and break away the mould in smaller portions. Experience is the best guide, however, and the student will soon learn how to chip round a form, and in the correct direction in which a chip should go. He will also learn that the chisel must not cut the plaster so much as crack it. The white portion should be easily removed if the first coloured part was well clay-watered. Having removed the white, the inner tinted mould must be chipped off. Needless to say this requires greater caution. If the design is of a complicated nature it is a good plan to keep the modelling alongside, whilst chipping, that is, if it came away from the mould in a recognisable condition, or should a drawing have been prepared, keep this handy. If often saves one from making a nasty gash if there is some such guide to refer to. When the mould has been chipped off, in all probability there will be cuts and scratches to repair. These are better if repaired with " killed " plaster (from which some of the virtue of the lime has been extracted). This is done by sprinkling the plaster into a vessel of water and allowing it to stand for some minutes untouched. Then stir as before, and apply with the tip of a brush. Have a bowl of clean water handy, and by keeping the thumb and fingers wet, this " killed " plaster may be modelled and smoothed imperceptibly into the surrounding plaster. Needless to say this should also be wet, otherwise it will absorb all the moisture from the plaster now applied, reducing it to a powder with no adhesive qualities. If necessary the surface of the cast may be worked upon with the steel tools, rifflers, files, and (sparingly) fine glass paper, but remember that the texture given to a modelling by the sweeps and touches of thumbs and fingers is far more interesting than the dead, uniform smoothness obtained by the other means. A few words of warning to the beginner. First test your plaster before attempting to cast any work you may value. Plasters vary in setting qualities : some set more quickly than others, and hence require to be used with greater expedition. Again, a little practice is necessary to find out the amount of plaster to use, as, if either too thick or too thin, the results are apt to be fatal. When removing the clay from the mould care must be exercised or pieces will break away from the mould. Don't hurry with the work at any stage, and if the plaster gets too thick to handle freely before you have used it, throw it away and mix some more. Proceed methodically, for often the beginner finds he has forgotten something, gets flurried and matters go from bad to worse, whereas, if he kept cool it is probable that the omission could easily be remedied.

CHAPTER IX.

CASTING A BUST.

THE student who has carried a bust to a satisfactory finish will naturally wish to see it in some more permanent material than clay. A cast in plaster is therefore made, even though the bust is to be reproduced in bronze or marble later on. The tools and materials are mentioned in the section devoted to casting a panel, the only addition being some Brunswick black for painting the iron composing the armature and some wooden wedges. A bust can usually be moulded in two pieces, one front and one back. The front portion is made first, and in order to get a clean edge a clay band is placed round the bust. The clay band is made by beating out a slab of clay to an even thickness of $\frac{1}{2}$ or $\frac{3}{4}$ of an inch, and cutting into strips about $1\frac{1}{2}$ inches wide. Having decided on the correct position for this band, remembering that the back portion of the mould is removed first and that it should draw easily without gripping the sides of the head or neck, you stick the band edgewise over the top of the head, behind the ears, and down the neck, to the base. Press this band well into contact with the modelling, and see that no gaps remain, or the plaster will ooze through. Continue the band round the stand in front of the bust about an inch away from the base to keep the plaster within bounds (Plate XVI. (a)). Arrange a few supports behind, to keep the band from washing away when the plaster is applied. Cover the back of the bust with tissue paper or newspaper, softened in water, to protect it from splashes. Gauge the amount of water you will require and into the bowl containing it pour some of the liquid colouring matter, avoiding sediment, or steep the blue bag in the clean water until coloured. Take the plaster up in the hands and allow it to trickle through the fingers, sprinkling it evenly over the water. Throw out all hard lumps. When the plaster begins to appear just below the surface of the water, stir briskly, keeping the spoon or hand well at the bottom, as the heavier plaster will settle down and is best reached by stirring low. The plaster should now be of the consistency of cream.

Applying the Plaster.—Dip some of the plaster out with the smaller bowl (being more easily handled) and throw it evenly on to the modelling. Begin at the top and, keeping the hand palm downwards, allow the plaster to slide off the fingers as the hand ascends. This imparts an upward impetus to the plaster, and if right in consistency, it will stay in place. If the plaster is thrown downwards it continues in this direction and slides smoothly to the base. See that the mixture enters all the cavities ; it will probably be necessary to blow it into the nostrils, eyes, ears, etc. This coat should be a very thin one, with the contours beneath readily discernible, except at the seam where it is built up until flush with the edge of the clay band (Plate XVI. (b)). A coating

(74)

PLATE XVI.

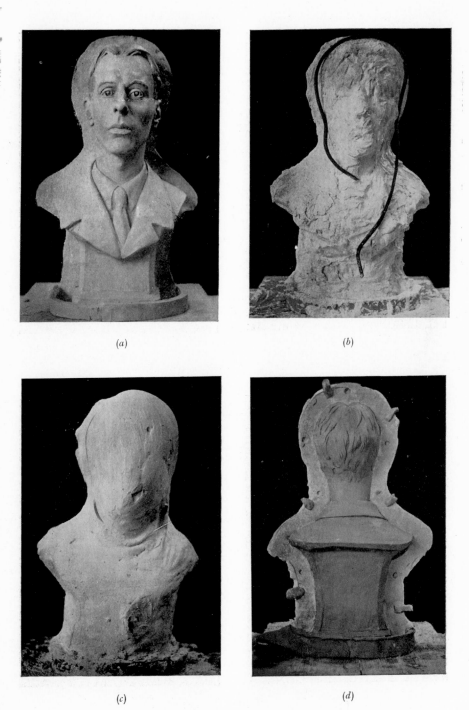

(a)

(b)

(c)

(d)

CASTING A BUST. THE MOULD.

PLATE XVII.

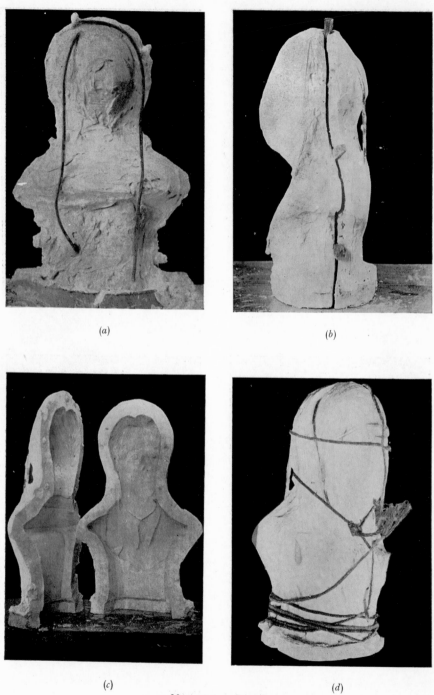

(a)

(b)

(c)

(d)

MOULDING A BUST.

of clay water is brushed over this coloured plaster, when set, so that the strengthening outer coat, when applied, will not adhere too firmly. Take a lump of soft clay in the left hand and press it into a cup shape ; pour a little water into this and rub with a fairly large brush. Paint this over the plaster. Bend an iron roughly to the contour of the mould and fix in position with a little plaster (see Plate XVI. (b)). We are now ready for the second coat. This should be four or five times as thick as the under one and not coloured. Gauge the amount of water required, sprinkle your plaster in, stir, and when properly mixed, throw on to the under coat. When it begins to set make the surface smooth and even, as it is stronger so than when rough and pitted (Plate XVI. (c)). When the front portion of the mould is complete, remove the clay band, thereby exposing the thickness of the mould. If there are any projections or inequalities on this edge smooth them away with the knife, and with the tip or a suitable tool excavate five or six shallow cavities. These, with the corresponding projections formed when the plaster of the back mould fills them, will form keys and will facilitate the fitting of the two portions together. Brush this edge well with clay-water, and stick a few lumps of clay at such portions of the mould as are strongest, and where you desire to insert the wedges used for separating (see Plate XVI. (d)).

Back Mould.—It is now ready for the back portion. Prepare a bowl of coloured plaster, as before, for the first thin coat. Bend and fit a length of iron rod into shape and position, fixing with a few lumps of plaster. Clay-water the surface of the coloured coat, and add the strengthening coat of white plaster (Plate XVII.). Make this coat smooth, and with the large knife cut away the plaster at the seam until a thin grey line appears, varied by the lumps of clay, indicating the spots for inserting the wedges.

Separating.—By this time the moulds should be set hard enough to stand separation. If, however, through excess of water or the poor quality of the plaster, it seems soft and spongy, leave it for awhile to harden. As the plaster sets it should become warm and give off a perceptible vapour. If this does not happen it is poor and will give trouble. It is wiser to test your plaster before commencing to cast an important work (especially if it has been kept for any length of time). But even new plasters vary considerably in setting qualities, some setting more quickly and requiring greater expedition in handling than others, so it is advisable to test it before attempting to cast. At all times, however, avoid thin plaster, as it is apt to be spongy, and chips badly, often with disastrous results to the cast. When you are satisfied that the mould is hard enough put the whole work in the sink and pour water over it. This does not affect the plaster, once set, but softens and expands the clay, making the separation of the moulds simpler. Insert the wooden wedges at the spots indicated by the clay and tap them sharply and evenly with the mallet. These wedges are better if made of hard wood as oak or pitchpine, because they keep their edges better when wet. They should be about 3 inches long and 1½ inches square, cut to an angle of 45° or thereabouts. As you drive the wedges home the seam will open (Plate XVII. (b)). Keep on pouring in water, and don't use too much force in pulling the back piece away. Don't hurry, for if the mould has caught on a projection in the bust the water poured in will soften the clay and loosen its grip. When the back portion of the mould is lifted away, proceed to cut the clay out of the front portion. With the knife carve a wedge-shaped piece out of the back and cut away on either side until the armature is freed. The mould can then be lifted off and the remainder of the clay removed. Plate XVII. (c) shows the two pieces of the mould. Always cut the clay away from the centre and ease the sides inwards away from the mould.

Preparing the Mould.—When all the clay is out, wash the mould thoroughly with the sponge and a soft brush. Sponge over the surface with soda-water, or pour in the soft soap in a liquid condition and allow to stand for awhile. Empty away, and wipe off with the sponge. Pour a few drops of olive or sweet oil into the palm of the left hand, if soap has been used, and having moistened the tip of a soft brush in the oil, paint over the surface until a diffused sheen appears. Thoroughly swill with clean water whether you have used soda, or soap and oil, and bind the two pieces together with a cord. The cord should be drawn as tightly as possible so that the moulds are in close contact at the seam. A few large wedges of wood inserted between the cord and the plaster helps to tighten ; and damping the cord also assists. Should there be any suspicious-looking gaps caulk them with soft clay and the mould is ready for pouring (Plate XVII (d)).

Pouring.—Mix enough plaster to coat the whole of the interior (white, of course) and, when ready, fix the mould head downwards and pour in. Turn the mould in all directions, so that the plaster reaches every part. When you have done this for a while, pour what has not adhered back into the bowl. Return again to the mould, and continue rolling the whole round to ensure an even coating, until the plaster begins to set. Mix another bowl of plaster and repeat the process until you feel sure that an even coating is given to the mould. Soak some tow, or coarse, wide-meshed canvas, in plaster, and spread it over the inside of the cast ; you may add a little more plaster to the base, if necessary, to ensure stability. Then, with a straight-edge, level the base until it is flush with the edges of the mould. The cord may now be taken off, and when a half an hour or so has elapsed, chipping commenced.

Chipping away the Mould.—For this purpose use very blunt chisels (as the plaster is cracked away rather than cut) and a mallet. The irons are taken out first, and then the outer coating chipped away. It is safer to commence at the top and work down, leaving the base and neck enclosed in the mould until the face and head are cleared, otherwise the jarring of this part may crack the neck. When the white coating has been removed, start on the coloured. Needless to say this requires greater care as any slip of the chisel is apt to penetrate the cast. Skill comes with experience and the student soon learns the best way to remove the mould. The white portion can often be lifted away in large pieces by inserting the chisel between it and the coloured part, but care must be exercised, or parts of the cast will come away too. Obviously, this method cannot be resorted to when removing the inner mould. This must be chipped off in such a manner that the pieces as they come away do not press against the nose, eyelids, or any other outstanding fragile parts. The chisel should be held vertical and tapped smartly with the mallet, watching all the time that you do not penetrate the cast. Practice is the best teacher, however, and the student will soon learn for himself the best way to chip. Plate XVIII. (a) shows the head and neck cleared. When the mould is removed it is probable that a few cuts and scratches will need repairing.

Repairing.—It is better to use " killed " plaster for this purpose : plaster from which some of the virtue of the lime has been extracted. If fresh plaster is used it will appear darker than the surrounding cast, and will also be harder, which is disconcerting if you endeavour to work over it with the plaster tools. For, whilst making hardly any impression on the repaired portions, the tool readily penetrates the softer cast and so renders the task of smoothing the surface a difficult one. To " kill " the plaster, sprinkle some into a vessel of water and allow to stand untouched for five minutes. Stir briskly and apply to the damaged parts with the tip of a brush, first wetting the part to be repaired. Have a bowl of clean water handy and by keeping the thumb and fingers thoroughly wet you may model the soft plaster and blend it into the surrounding surface.

Replacing Broken Portions.—Should a portion of the nose, or an eyelid, ear, or part of the hair have broken off, soak the piece in water, and well saturate the part from which it has broken. Mix some fresh plaster, and apply to the edges to be united, press the piece firmly into place and hold until set. It is fatal to move in the slightest, especially when the plaster is about to set. When you have repaired all the chips on the surface of the cast, scrape away the seam, and, if necessary, work over the face with the steel tools, rifflers, files (and sparingly), fine glass-paper. But do as little of this as possible, for the texture given by the sweeps and touches of thumb and fingers is far more interesting than the dead, smooth quality obtained by working on the plaster. Plate XVIII. (b) is the finished cast.

CHAPTER X.

CASTING A FIGURE IN THE ROUND.

CASTING a figure in the round requires a little more care and thought than casting a bust. It is rarely possible to cast even the simplest of poses with a mould of less than three pieces. Usually more are required. This, of course, applies to waste moulding, for piece moulding is far more complex, and rather beyond the scope of this book.

Arranging Pieces.—The first consideration in casting a figure is the arrangement of the pieces composing the mould. They must be fitted in such a way that it is possible to remove all the clay, and at the same time clear the supporting iron. This iron which usually enters the figure at the base of the vertebral column necessitates a break in the mould at this part. So the back of the figure is invariably moulded in two pieces, whilst the front, if possible, is made in one piece, and to this piece the others are fitted. It is better to have one piece the whole length of the figure, to which smaller pieces may be fitted, as this ensures a cast identical in pose to the clay figure. When you have decided how to divide the mould, the clay bands determining the pieces are prepared. Beat out a slab of clay about an inch thick, rather more for a large figure and less for a small one, and when perfectly smooth and even cut it into strips from $1\frac{1}{2}$ to 2 inches wide. Commencing at the head and working down the figure you press these bands edgewise into close contact with the model, remembering that the front portion is moulded first, but the back portions removed first. Such being the case it is better to keep the clay bands well back on the figure so that the hinder portion of the mould will " pull " freely without gripping the sides of the head, neck, trunk, or limbs. For if this happens and the clay is at all hard, there is a danger of breaking the edges of the mould. Behind the ears, and well back on the neck, shoulders, arms, body, and legs is the best position for the seam (Plate XVIII. (c)). Take your time over fitting the band, and see that no spaces are left between it and the figure, or the plaster will ooze through. Fit some wedge-shaped supports behind the clay wall to prevent the plaster from washing it away. Cover the back with tissue paper or newspaper, softened with water, to keep off the splashes when you throw on the plaster for the front mould.

Coloured Coat.—It is now ready for the plaster. The first coat is coloured to facilitate chipping. In the previous sections I have suggested that all materials should be ready to hand before commencing operations. We will assume that some powder—colour, yellow ochre, raw sienna, or similar earth colour—has been dissolving in a vessel of water. In the large bowl carefully gauge the amount of water necessary to mix the plaster for a thin coat over the front of the work. Experience is the best guide, but it is decidedly annoying

(78)

PLATE XVIII.

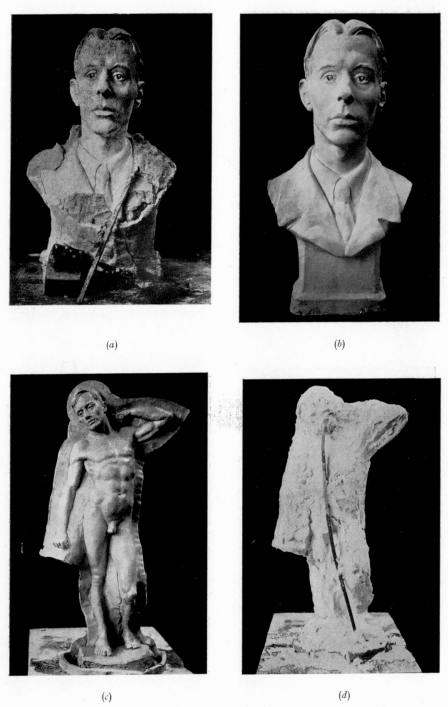

(a)

(b)

(c)

(d)

CASTING A BUST AND A FIGURE.

PLATE XIX.

(a)

(b)

(c)

(d)

CASTING A FIGURE. THE MOULD.

to find that you have insufficient plaster for your purpose. It is better to have too much than too little. Into the clean water you have measured, pour some of the colouring matter above mentioned, avoiding sediment. Or, more handy still, steep a blue bag in the bowl until sufficient colour has dissolved. It is only necessary that you should be able to differentiate between this plaster and the white when chipping away the mould. Into this coloured water sprinkle the plaster, by allowing it to trickle between the fingers until you see it appear evenly just below the surface of the water. Should your bowl contain too much water pour away until you see the wet plaster beginning to run away too, which will not occur until the thinner water has cleared off. I have known casters who always poured the water from the top of the plaster, and it certainly ensures against getting too thin a mixture. Needless to say, a few minutes have been allowed for the plaster to soak, and in either case, whether you pour off the superflous water, or add enough plaster to soak it all up, it is better to allow a few minutes before stirring. It ensures a more even mixture and greater freedom from lumps. Now thrust the spoon, or hand, well down in the bowl and stir briskly from side to side until the whole mixture is even in consistency and free from lumps. Dip some of the plaster out with the smaller bowl (being easier to handle) and commence throwing on to the figure.

Applying the Plaster.—Begin at the head, allowing the plaster to fall from the fingers, as you jerk the hand upwards with the palm down. This imparts an upward impetus to the plaster, which operates against its natural downward tendency and helps to keep it in place. Blow the plaster into the cavities, and see that every part is covered, for upon the way this coating fits the clay your cast will depend. Keep this coat of plaster thin, about a quarter of an inch, except at the seams, where it is built up to the height of the clay band, to ensure uniformity at the seams, instead of a disconcerting mixture of coloured and white (Plate XVIII. (a)). Allow this to set and then brush well over with clay water, so that, when chipping, the outer coating will leave freely. To do this take a lump of soft clay in the left hand, and hollow it into a cup shape. Pour some water into the hollow and rub a brush into the clay and water. It will be necessary to strengthen the mould with an iron rod to keep it from warping. Take a rod of iron half an inch square in section, and bend it roughly into shape. Fix it with a few blobs of plaster and it is ready for the outer coating (Plate XVIII.).

Outer Coating.—This outer coating of white plaster should be four or five times as thick as the under, coloured, one. If the bowl is not large enough to mix the whole lot at once, it may be applied in two or three coatings, but each should be added before the under ones are set hard. Mix the plaster as before and apply fairly quickly, and when the final coat is beginning to set, smooth the surface with the hands, as it is much stronger so than when rough and uneven. For the mould is only as strong as its thinnest portion.

Back Moulds.—It is now ready for the back moulds. Remove the clay band from the edge and the paper from the lower half of the back, as this lower half is better made first. Scrape away any roughness and inequalities from the edge of the mould and bore some holes to form keys. Arrange another band of clay across the middle of the figure, on a level with the support where it enters the model. Stick a few lumps of clay to the edge of the mould where you wish to insert your wedges and paint the whole edge with clay water (Plate XIX. (b)). Gauge the amount of water required, add the colour and mix as before. Apply this mixture to the figure in a thin coat, building up at the seam to the level of the front mould (Plate XIX. (c)). Clay-water, fix the strengthening iron in position, and add the outer coating of white plaster (Plate XIX. (d)). When this is set, scrape away from the seam until a thin grey line appears, varied by the clay, indicating the spots for the wedges. The top portion has now to be made. Clear away the bands of clay, and remove the paper. Mix the necessary quantity of coloured plaster and apply. Brush over with clay-water, fix the iron in position and add the final coat of white plaster as before (Plate XIX.). When set carve the plaster from the seam, and the mould is ready for separating.

Separating Mould.—See that the mould is hard before you commence and do not hurry. When you are satisfied that it is set sufficiently hard, place the whole in the sink and pour water over it. Insert the wedges at the spots indicated by the lumps of clay, in the upper half of the mould, and tap gently with the mallet. Give each wedge a tap in turn until you see the seam open, pouring water over the whole time. When the seam opens pour more water into the opening and gradually ease off the top half of the back mould. Don't force it off, for if it has caught on the clay, and the latter is at all hard, your plaster is liable to break. Ease it off gently, applying plenty of water, as this will soften the clay and loosen its grip. When the top piece is free, pour on more water and ease off the lower piece in the same way.

Clearing the Mould.—The back of the clay figure is now exposed whilst the front is still encased in plaster. Take the knife and cut a wedge of clay from the back, and continue cutting from the sides until the armature is exposed (Plate XX.). Treat the limbs in the same way and the armature can be freed. Lay the mould flat and force the remaining clay inwards towards the centre of the mould until you have cleared it all away. Take care that no clay remains in the ears, or outstanding parts of the hair, for being difficult to see, this is often left, and will require building up in plaster later on. Thoroughly cleanse the mould, by washing with clean water, the sponge, and a soft brush. Pour in some soda-water and sponge well over to ensure that every part has been reached. Treat the other portions of the mould in a similar manner, then pour off the soda-water. If soap and oil are preferred, proceed as indicated in the description given of casting a bust.

Armature of Iron Rods.—The armature of iron rods has now to be fixed. Cut some lengths of half-inch square rod and bend to shape. A long one from the head well down into the base by way of the standing leg, another for the bent leg, and one or two for the arms, according to the pose. It is sometimes possible to take one iron across the chest and down each arm to the hand, and, where possible, this arrangement makes for strength. Often two irons are necessary, one for each arm. Fit these irons carefully into the front half of the mould, and see that they are free of the back portions, when the latter are laid in position. When you are satisfied that the irons fit nicely, heat them and brush over with Brunswick black. This is to prevent them from rusting and discolouring the cast. When dry, fix them into position in the front mould with a few lumps of fresh plaster (Plate XX.). This must be carefully done, as the irons must not come into contact with the mould, neither must the plaster used to keep them in position block up the channels through which the liquid plaster is to be poured when filling the mould. They must also be firmly fixed, or the shaking that takes place later may dislodge them, with disastrous

Plate XX.

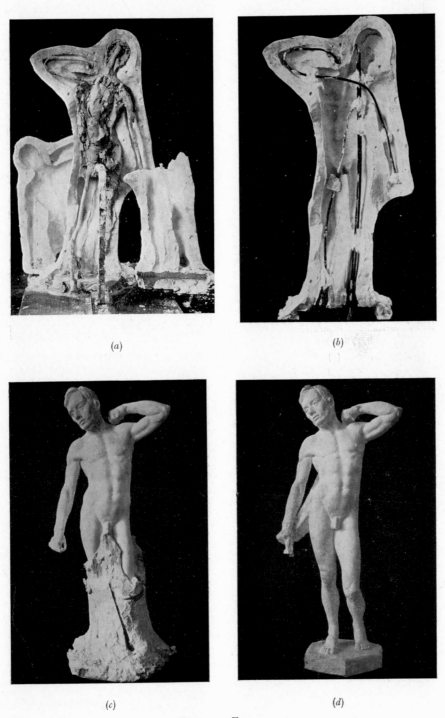

(a)

(b)

(c)

(d)

Casting a Figure.

PLATE XXI.

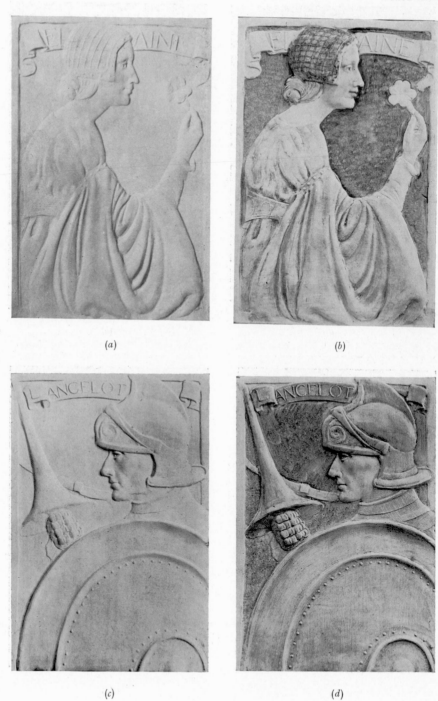

(a)

(b)

(c)

(d)

COLOURED LOW RELIEFS.

results. Allow the plaster to set before moving the mould, then give it a final swill with clean water, and after treating the other portions in the same manner, fit the pieces together. Bind securely with cord, until the seams are just thin lines and the portions of the mould in close contact. Some large wedges forced between the cord and mould aids in tightening ; and damping the cord is of still further assistance. Should there be any gaps, caulk them with clay ; there will be at least one, where the iron support passed through.

Filling the Mould.—The mould is now ready for filling. Stand the mould, head downwards and mix a large bowl of plaster ; stir thoroughly until free from lumps, then pour slowly into the mould through the hollows representing the feet. Keep shaking the mould, or bubbles may form ; and turn it about in all directions to ensure that the plaster reaches every part. Having emptied the bowl, place it just below the opening in the mould (or better still, get someone to hold it for you) and allow the plaster to run back into the bowl again. Revolve the mould so that the plaster pours out from each side in turn. As soon as it ceases to flow from the mould, return it again as soon as possible. Keep turning all the while, and if not too hard, run the plaster out again, and back again, until it is too stiff to run. If the mould has not been filled by this first mixing, prepare some more as quickly as you can, and pour until the mould fills up level with the edges at the base. As it begins to set, smooth off any inequalities with a straight-edge so that you will have a flat base for the figure to stand on. This will, of course, give a solid cast ; a hollow one is difficult to make, and should not be attempted by the beginner. Allow the plaster to set for half an hour, then remove the cord and commence chipping.

Chipping.—Clear the irons away first, after which chip off the white part of the mould. Commence at the top and work down. It is safer to leave the legs in the mould until the top part is clear, otherwise the jarring consequent upon the chipping of the upper portions may break them. Again, chip out the head, whilst the neck is still supported in the mould. There are always some parts of the mould which are better chipped first, and other portions which are better left for awhile, but it depends upon the figure, and the student soon learns which to take first and which to leave (Plate XX.). Don't hurry with the chipping, and remember that the mould is cracked and not cut. " Don't hurry " is a good motto for the caster, patience and care are very essential, and if anything should go wrong, or anything be forgotten, don't get flustered, for this generally leads to further trouble, but calmly set about righting the matter. There are very few accidents likely to occur to even a beginner (if he is careful) that cannot be remedied when taken calmly. Perhaps the worst thing that can happen is a mould too soft to handle, the result of carelessness in mixing, or in not testing the plaster before commencing—carelessness anyway. Plate XX. (d) is the finished cast.

7

CHAPTER XI.

GELATINE AND WAX MOULDING.

WHEN a number of casts are required of a work in the round, or of one which is undercut, a gelatine mould is often employed instead of the more complicated " piece mould " of plaster. The elastic quality of gelatine allows it to be pulled from beneath projections, and around bulging surfaces, after which it immediately springs back to its proper position. As a moulding material it is, therefore, of great value if used skilfully. It is extensively employed in producing plaster work for commercial purposes. The gelatine should be of good quality. Glue is sometimes employed but it does not keep so well or produce such good casts as gelatine. The best way to prepare the gelatine is to soak in cold water until quite soft, when it is placed into a saucepan or other suitable vessel, and dissolved slowly over a very gentle flame. It is safer to melt it in a vessel of water similar to a glue-pot as the direct application of the heat to the vessel containing the gelatine is liable to burn it, thereby destroying its elasticity and setting qualities. When it is melted remove it from the heat and stir thoroughly but gently. Allow it to stand until a thin skin forms over the surface, and it is possible to grasp the outside of the vessel without discomfort. It should be possible to keep the finger in the gelatine without being burned, before it is poured over the model. If it is a panel we are moulding, it will be necessary to frame the work with strips of clay or wood, as in the case of plaster moulding, to keep the gelatine from running about. First of all, however, the panel must be coated with shellac to keep the gelatine from adhering. If the model is of plaster there will be no difficulty in coating it with shellac, but if of clay it must be allowed to harden somewhat so that the surface is fairly dry when the shellac is applied. It is not necessary for all the moisture to dry out, as there is a tendency in the clay to crack and crumble when dry. It should be hard enough to allow of brushing over without disturbing the surface, and dry enough to take the shellac. A cast which has been waxed will not require a coat of shellac, as the wax serves the purpose quite as well. Linseed oil may also be used but is not so good as shellac.

Moulding.—The panel having been protected with shellac, wax, or linseed oil, and the walls erected to keep the gelatine within bounds, if the gelatine is sufficiently cool it may be poured gently over the surface. Care should be taken to see that it enters all the interstices of the modelling and also that no air-bubbles form. Allow this to set, and then after brushing over with a solution of alum, or 1½ ozs. of sugar of lead (acetate) and 2 ozs. of brown sugar dissolved in a strong solution of alum, give it a backing of plaster. When set remove the plaster backing, and gently ease the gelatine mould away from the model. Do not hurry this or attempt to force the two apart or the mould may tear.   If there is a tendency to stick, plunge the whole into water.   When the mould is removed, brush the surface with the alum or other solution, wipe with a soft rag, and finally brush over with crude petroleum, or with paraffin and French chalk mixed to the consistency of cream.   Place the gelatine into position on the backing of plaster and pour in the plaster for the cast.

WAX MOULDING.

Composition of Wax.—Moulding wax is composed of beeswax, 1 part, powdered resin, 1 to 2 parts, melted together with a small proportion of tallow. The quantity of tallow depends upon the quality of the wax.   If the mould is to be made from a clay model it is only necessary to erect a fence round the panel as in the case of plaster and gelatine moulding, and to pour the wax over when it is of the right consistency.   It should be just liquid enough to pour easily, not too hot and, needless to say, not too cold, or it will pour badly or not at all.   If the model is of plaster it should be allowed to absorb as much water as it will hold, and the surface sponged dry before pouring on the wax.   As the wax cools a coating will form over the modelling, which should be allowed to thicken until from $\frac{1}{4}$ inch to 1 inch (according to the size of the work) has formed and the rest poured off.   A backing of plaster is then added.

When set the plaster is removed and the wax gently eased off.   If it adheres to the model it may be plunged into warm water which makes it more elastic and easier to draw.   Clean the mould and fill with plaster as with gelatine and plaster moulding.

CHAPTER XII.

MOULDING A BUST IN GELATINE.

MOULDING a bust in gelatine is not difficult if proper attention is paid to the heat and consistency of the gelatine and to the preparation of the mould-case. Assuming we have a plaster bust of which we need some replicas, we first give it a coating of shellac. When this has hardened, beat some clay out into a sheet of from 1 inch to 1½ inches thick, and lay it in an even coat over the whole of the bust. This clay will ultimately be replaced by gelatine so care should be exercised to ensure the necessary thickness over the whole surface. Over this coating of clay plaster is thrown, which, when set, will form the containing case into which the gelatine is fitted when a cast is required. This case is made in two pieces (front and back) similar to those described in casting a bust by the waste mould process. A clay band is laid edgewise over the top and down either side to the base. See description and figures illustrating " Casting a Bust." Mix a bowl of plaster (without colour) and cover the front half of the clay, keeping it thicker at the clay band (where the seam will come). When this has set remove the clay band, smooth the edge of the plaster and brush over with clay-water. Gouge a few holes to serve as keys, and then cover the back with plaster. Allow this to set, after which the front half of the case should be drawn carefully away, leaving the back in position. Remove the clay from this part of the bust, leaving the clay over the back still in place. Cut it evenly around the edge of the plaster and see that no gaps remain into which the gelatine can percolate. Shellac the front part of the case (inside) and the exposed edge of clay, to keep the gelatine from sticking. Replace the case, fitting it closely against the back piece, and tie them firmly together. Before doing this, however, it is advisable to bore a couple of holes through, one fairly low down and the other at about the level of the nose, or any other convenient spot. When tied, caulk the seam with clay or plaster, as the gelatine has a marked tendency to ooze through the most minute gaps. Now invert the whole work, gently and cautiously, or the bust will move inside the case. If it is allowed to lean backwards slightly towards the clay still remaining in the case, the danger is minimised. Instead of inverting, the following plan is sometimes adopted. A third piece of plaster is fitted over the base, in a manner similar to that used for the other two, and a funnel-shaped hole bored at the top of the head (in the case) through which the gelatine is poured.

Pouring.—Having fixed the bust in position (inverted) the gelatine is melted, and allowed to cool, for if too hot it will dissolve the protecting coat of shellac and adhere to the plaster. It should not be too hot to bear the finger in. Now pour it gently into the space between the front of the bust and the outside case. For this purpose a funnel is useful. When the gelatine rises to the level of the first hole, it should be stopped with clay, and more gelatine added until the next hole is reached, which must also be stopped, and the pouring continued until the mould is full. The purpose served by the holes is to allow the air to escape easily and also to give an idea of how the mould is filling, *i.e.* whether the gelatine is escaping anywhere. Allow the gelatine to harden, then carefully remove the back portion of the plaster case and the clay, leaving the edge of the gelatine mould exposed. Treat this with the alum solution, and coat the inside of the plaster case with shellac. Bore a couple of holes in the case similar to those in the front half and tie the two halves firmly in place, caulking the seams. When the gelatine is sufficiently cool, fill up this part of the mould, stopping the holes as the liquid rises to their respective levels. If the gelatine is too hot at this stage it will melt the edge of the front portion, and the seam in the final cast will be unsightly.

Separating.—Now leave the mould for a couple of hours to set thoroughly, after which the outer case may be separated, and the mould gradually eased away from the bust. Brush it over with the alum or other solution, wipe with a soft rag, and finally brush with crude petroleum, or, with paraffin and French chalk mixed to the consistency of cream. Put the gelatine back into its place in the plaster case, fit the whole together and bind firmly. It only remains now to pour in the plaster as described in the section devoted to "Casting a Bust"

CHAPTER XIII.

BRONZING, COLOURING, AND WAXING PLASTER CASTS.

PLASTER is always a disappointing material to look upon after clay, for though the reproduction of the modelling may be absolute, the dead white of the plaster lacks the inimitable quality of the clay. There are methods of treating the plaster, however, whereby the deadly opacity of the surface may be to some extent veiled, with a corresponding improvement in its appearance, and also in its dirt-resisting capacity. For plaster unprotected is easily soiled, and its dirty white surface when in this condition looks very poor and unpleasant.

Shellac.—The simplest method of treating the surface is to brush the cast over with white shellac dissolved in methylated spirit. This preparation or " French polish," as it is often called, is quite simple. A few lumps of white shellac (not brown) are dropped into a bottle containing methylated spirit and allowed to dissolve. The bottle should be kept stoppered, as the spirit is very volatile. The plaster must be perfectly clean and dry. It is a good plan to keep the cast covered up whilst drying, as the dust that accumulates and the finger marks that inevitably appear are unpleasantly obtrusive, even when shellacked. Should the cast be dirty, it will be necessary to clean it before applying the shellac. If it is merely a surface layer of dust, it may be possible to remove it with a duster or by blowing, or even with fine glass-paper, provided the surface modelling is not interfered with. Should these methods prove unsuccessful the cast will need to be washed. By washing I do not mean wiped over with a damp sponge or cloth, for this would be fatal. The dirt that was previously only on the surface will permeate with the moisture from the sponge ; becoming difficult, if not impossible, to remove from the plaster. The only way to cleanse the cast is to immerse it completely in water, and allow it to remain untouched until it has absorbed all the water it is capable of holding. When the bubbles cease to rise, and when on being removed from the water the surface remains wet, it should be returned to the water and wiped over with a clean sponge, which will detach the dirt and leave it floating in the water. If the sponge is used before the plaster is saturated the dirt will be absorbed, and, as before stated, will be impossible to get rid of. Needless to say, the plaster must be allowed to dry thoroughly before the shellac is applied.

BRONZING.

Provide yourself with an ounce or so of brown shellac, and dissolve it in methylated spirit. Some powder colours, burnt umber, raw umber, emerald green, and, if desired, a little lampblack, and even reds and blues if a purple tinge is desired. A few fairly large hog-hair brushes, a couple of saucers, some

(86)

bronze powder, red and gold, and some cotton wool, completes the list.   When perfectly dry give the cast a coating of shellac.   Brush this over freely, taking care to cover the whole surface, and at the same time avoid brushing over the same spot too often as it disturbs the film of shellac, which forms very rapidly. Allow this coating to harden thoroughly, say half an hour, before applying the next.   For the second coating take some of the powder colour, either the raw or burnt umber, according to whether you desire a warm red bronze or a cool, greenish one, and place it on one side of a saucer.   Pour some of the shellac into the other portion of the saucer and stir sufficient of the powder colour into the shellac to coat the plaster a uniform brown.   It should be fluid enough to flow freely over the cast, and should be floated on as quickly and directly as possible.   Avoid brushing over the second time whilst the mixture is setting as it is easily disturbed.   Allow this sufficient time to harden, and, if necessary, give it another coat.   If, however, you are satisfied with the colour, you may mix a little of the bronze powder with shellac and apply it to such portions of the cast as you desire.   Generally, the projecting parts are the most likely to take a polish, and the bronze powder is better confined to these areas.   The gold bronze may be used alone, if desired, but a little of the red bronze added helps to suggest the copper that enters so largely into the composition of bronze. The application of this bronze powder requires care and thought, as too much looks somewhat vulgar, whilst isolated patches are apt to appear artificial. The emerald green is now brushed on with equal care and consideration.   This colour is to represent the patina which lends such a charm to old bronze, and naturally collects in the hollows and such portions as are not exposed.   It is essential that you should have a definite idea of the type of bronze you wish to imitate, and, if possible, it is well to have a specimen of actual bronze handy. When these applications have hardened it may be an improvement to brush over certain portions again with the umber, or you may wish to add a little more bronze or green.   You will learn by experiment what to do and how to do it. It is now time to give the work a coating of wax, as described under " Waxing." Brush this over and leave for half a day for the turpentine to evaporate, after which it may be polished with a pad of cotton wool or soft linen.   This fixes the pigments that are dissolved in shellac, and should you desire to make any further alterations in the colour of the bronze, it can easily and safely be done after waxing, by using the colour and shellac as before.   A further coat of wax, allowed to set, and afterwards polished completes the process.   The bust illustrated in Plate IX. (c) and (d) was treated in this way.

Coating with Bronze Powder.—Another method of Procedure is to coat the cast with bronze powder after the first protective coating of shellac has been allowed to harden.   The cast will now appear like a cheap imitation of gold, and altogether inartistic, but when the shellac has hardened the umber (raw or burnt) is brushed over as before.   By leaving the colour fairly opaque in the hollows, and wiping off the exposed portions with a soft rag, a good suggestion of bronze is obtained.   The succeeding stages are similar to those previously described, the only difference being that the bronze powder is applied first instead of the umber.   Instead of using shellac, for floating on the colour, after the bronze powder has been applied with shellac, gold size thinned with turpentine may be used as a medium.   Oil colour may be used in a similar manner, thinned with turpentine, as if used too thick it is apt to blur the modelling.

Still another method is to coat the plaster with boiled oil, adding when the surface is dry a further coating of terebine. Over this, when hard, the shellac and colour is applied as before. The coating of bronze colour obtained by either of the foregoing methods is very thin, and consequently liable to chip off when knocked, leaving the white plaster exposed in objectionable patches. This may be obviated by painting over with a black water-stain or ink, prior to coating with shellac. This goes more deeply into the plaster, and the chipped parts are therefore less obvious.

WAXING.

White plaster, as previously stated, is rather too dead in appearance to be entirely pleasant to look upon, besides which it is easily soiled. When treated with wax, however, especially if a little colouring matter is added, it can be made to assume a delicate ivory tint more interesting than the dead white, and not so easily soiled. The plaster must be thoroughly dry and clean before the wax is applied. The wax should be of good quality stearine or white paraffin wax. This is dissolved in turpentine by heating together until a fairly liquid mixture, easy to manipulate, has been obtained. A lump of wax sufficiently large for the purpose is shredded into a jar containing turpentine, which is placed in a saucepan of water, and heated until the wax dissolves. The saucepan of water is a precautionary measure, for turpentine, being highly inflammable, it is necessary to keep the flame from it. Half a pint of turpentine to a lump of wax about three times the size of a walnut is about the proportion, but a little experience is the best guide. If the turpentine preponderates, the cast will soak up a lot before the surface is affected, whereas if the mixture is too stiff it is apt to clog.

Applying the Wax.—The dissolved wax is applied with a brush, fairly large, taking care to cover the whole surface as evenly as possible. If the cast is slightly warm the wax will spread more evenly. The wax itself should be kept hot by allowing it to remain in the saucepan of hot water, for when cool it clogs the surface of the modelling. Should this occur, hold the cast near the fire until the mixture becomes fluid again. When sufficient has been absorbed the face of the cast will assume a dull polish which can be heightened by rubbing briskly but lightly with a pad of cotton wool or soft linen rag. Should the effect desired be a dull ivory, a little powder, yellow ochre, raw umber, and black may be added to the mixture and applied with the brush just before giving the final polish. Rub well into the hollows, and wipe off such portions as you wish to remain light. This darkening of the hollows and lightening of raised portions enhances the modelling, and helps considerably to give the appearance of old ivory. Rub briskly with the soft pad, and if a fairly high polish is desired, dust a little French chalk over before rubbing. For more elaborate colour effects, see instructions for colouring plaster.

CHAPTER XIV.

COLOURED PLASTER.

A LOW relief in plaster to which colour has been applied possesses a decorative quality distinctly its own. The delicate charm of the relief, with its subtle lights and shades is emphasised by the addition of flat tints, provided the latter are harmonious. It also increases its visibility, for a panel on which the highest relief is no more than half an inch will be visible at a hundred feet when coloured, as against fifty feet when uncoloured.

Design.—The design must be specially planned when the work is to be coloured, with good, bold shapes and simple modelling. From the outset it should be recognised that colour and relief are each to play their part in producing the effect, and the design prepared accordingly. Large plain shapes contrasted with shapes more broken and detailed, where the colour will vary from a pale tint on the projections to a deeper hue in the cavities, will make for variety and interest. A good plan is to prepare the scheme on brown paper with charcoal and white chalk before modelling. The colour may be thought out in a separate sketch with pastel or water-colour. For the relief the chalk and charcoal on brown paper (or tinted paper) works very well, as the paper serves for the general tone, whilst the shadows are suggested by the charcoal, and the lights by the chalk. A good idea of the relief can be obtained by this method, and if the design is made the same size as the panel, it can be transferred to the clay background by tracing with a hard point. If, however, this is impracticable, the drawing should be squared, with corresponding squares on the clay and the enlargement made so.

Preparing Ground.—The ground should present a perfectly smooth surface, as it is easier to draw upon, and also gives a definite plane upon which to build your relief. The more subtle the relief the greater the need for a level ground. It should be prepared by nailing strips of wood to the board (to serve as a frame) and, having damped the board and pressed the clay well into contact with it, level the surface with a straight-edge. The frame will enable you to obtain a level surface flush with its upper edge.

Modelling.—Having prepared the ground and drawn your design upon it, proceed to build up your relief, keeping it as subtle and delicate as you like, provided the edges bounding the shapes are well defined. For the colour when applied will accumulate at these edges and give further emphasis to the shapes. When your relief is finished a mould is made (see "Casting" section) and any details that may be necessary added in the mould. The lettering on the two panels illustrated (Plate XXI.) was incised in the mould, together with the studs on the shield, the head dress of "Elaine," and other fine details. Having finished your work in the mould, take a cast, and allow it to dry thoroughly. It is then treated with size, wax, or shellac, as otherwise the

surface will be absorbent and will soak up the colour before you can distribute
it.　If size is used it must be perfectly clear, fairly fluid, and applied with
a good sized brush, until absorption ceases.　Wax is better, but has a
tendency to work up when the colour is added.　But if carefully done the
wax method is capable of producing very beautiful effects.　The wax, stearine
or white paraffin wax, is dissolved in turpentine as described in the section on
" Waxing," and applied with a brush until the surface of the plaster ceases to
absorb.　The wax must be kept hot, and the cast should be warmed to make
it work evenly.　When sufficient has been absorbed the plaster will assume an
eggshell gloss.　The shellac (white) is dissolved in methylated spirit and applied
until the surface has a slight sheen.　Each coat should be allowed to set before
applying the next, and the final coat takes the colour better if allowed to become
thoroughly hard.　Either of these preparations may then be worked over with
oil colour, thinned with turpentine in transparent washes.　Or in the case of
the wax powder colour may be ground and thoroughly mixed with the turpentine
and wax.　In all cases brush the colour lightly over the surface and, where
desired, wipe off with a soft rag or pad of cotton wool.　Remember that the
colour must be transparent, and as thin as possible, for a thick coating of pigment destroys the character of the work and looks dull and heavy.　The charm
lies in the semi-transparency of the colour which may be allowed to settle in the
hollows, and wiped from the projecting parts with good results.　White paint
should be eschewed, the white plaster will serve for the lights far better than
a heavy coating of opaque pigment (Plate XXI.).

CHAPTER XV.

FIBROUS PLASTER.

FIBROUS plaster is used extensively for interior decoration. It is tough, durable, and easily handled. The work is first modelled in clay, with due regard for its ultimate position and setting, after which a mould is made in plaster, gelatine, or wax. Of these gelatine is most frequently employed, as, being elastic and pliable, it " pulls " or leaves the cast more easily than wax or plaster. For low relief work with no " undercutting " the two last-mentioned materials may safely be used. When the gelatine mould has been made (see Gelatine Casting) the surface is brushed over with a fairly strong solution of alum, or the following preparation : Dissolve $1\frac{1}{2}$ ozs. of sugar of lead (acetate) and 2 ozs. of brown sugar in 1 quart of strong alum solution. After brushing over with either of these preparations wipe the surface dry, and oil with crude petroleum, or with a mixture of paraffin and French chalk about the consistency of cream. The mould is then covered to about $\frac{1}{8}$ inch with plaster gauged with clean water. The second coat (applied before the first one has set) is gauged with size water, which retards the setting and at the same time toughens the plaster. The size water is made with glue of good quality. Into this second coating of plaster are placed the strengthening materials. Lathes of thin wood, tow, coarse, open-meshed canvas known as " scrim," galvanised wire, and even wire netting are used for this purpose. The " scrim " must be well saturated with plaster and thoroughly incorporated with the second coating or there is a danger of separation. The lathes, wire, or other strengtheners are pressed well into the plaster to ensure a good grip. For small casts, where " scrim " would be too coarse and clumsy, fine butter muslin is employed. The advantage of fibrous plaster is, that it may be cast into very thin light slabs, which are readily applied to wall surfaces and ceilings, are easily handled, and less liable to fracture than casts that are made from plaster alone.

CHAPTER XVI.

LETTERING.

LETTERING is frequently needed by the student of modelling for inscriptions on memorial tablets, for mottoes and quotations introduced into schemes of decoration, etc. If the letters are poor in form, or awkward in spacing they detract from, instead of adding to, the beauty of the work. The decorative quality of Roman lettering with its wonderful variety of thick and thin, curved and straight lines, must assuredly add to the beauty of any work if well drawn and tastefully introduced. Study the forms from the inscription on the Trajan column, and base your letters upon them. Remember that the first essential in lettering is that it shall be readable, so that fantastic forms are to be strenuously avoided.

Incised Lettering.—Plate XXII. (*a*), (*b*), and (*c*) illustrates an alphabet incised on a slab of plaster. The slab in this case was cast on a sheet of glass to ensure a smooth, even surface. The lettering was drawn on paper, which was placed on the plaster, as soon as the latter had set, and traced through with a firm point : a knitting needle serves very well. A moderate pressure is sufficient to impress the forms of the letters through the paper on to the surface of the plaster. They were then incised with bone tools filed to the requisite shape. Boxwood tools may be used but are liable to lose their shape after scraping the plaster for awhile. Steel or brass are also good, the brass being more easily filed to shape than the steel. The section of the letters is V shaped. For stone or marble the inscription can be traced through by inserting a sheet of carbon paper between the drawing and the stone before using the point. The letters are then incised with chisels of correct shape and a hammer or mallet. For inscriptions on stone or marble the incised letter is eminently suitable, being the most easily executed.

Raised Lettering.—Raised lettering necessitates the cutting away of the background to a uniform depth, leaving the forms of the letters standing in relief. For this method great care is required as the stone is easily chipped and once chipped the piece cannot be replaced.

In bronze, raised lettering has a much richer appearance than incised. When preparing the model for bronze casting it is a fairly simple matter to raise the lettering by incising it in the mould, as it will then be raised in the final cast. The inscription is drawn on the clay, the best plan being to draw the letters on paper, place the paper in position on the clay and trace through with a hard point, a similar method to that already described for incised lettering on the slab of plaster. The forms will appear on the clay in a sort of blurred line, which will be quite distinct in the plaster mould, which should now be made. The letters in the mould will be reversed, and the outlines which were incised

(92)

on the clay will now appear raised.   This procedure is much simpler than trying
to draw the letters reversed in the mould, for not only are the letters reversed
but the inscription would have to be spaced from right to left instead of from
left to right.   The method used here does all the changing necessary in letters
and spacing, and leaves them in the mould all ready for incising.   Now prepare
a couple of tools of bone, brass, or some other easily filed but fairly hard material, with which to cut into the mould.   One for the thick strokes, another for
the narrow, and a sharper one for the points of the serifs, will be enough and
will help to make the letters uniform.   Remember that you are working in the
mould and that there must be no undercutting or the letters when cast will not
" pull " easily, but will adhere to the mould.   It is not wise either to get them
too great in projection, for the same reason.   Plate XXII. (b) illustrates raised
letters which were cut in the mould.

CHAPTER XVII.

TILES.

Cloisonne, or raised line tiles, depend for their effect upon patches of coloured glazes enclosed by a raised line. The first consideration when designing for this process is the shapes and sizes of the patches of colour composing the tile. Prepare the design on paper, allowing for shrinkage. Tiles are usually 6 inches square when finished, but as they shrink somewhat in firing, it is advisable to allow for this in the design. Set out a square of 6¼ inch sides, and plan the design within this square, taking into consideration the nature of the " repeat," and the purpose and position of the tile when finished. It is better to sketch the main lines of the design in three or four squares first, after you have decided upon the nature of the " repeat," *i.e.* whether " side by side," " drop," or " brickwise." This is to ensure correct repetition, and also to give some idea of the ultimate effect. Shapes of colour, bounded by a line of lighter colour, are the elements with which we are to make our design. It is essential, then,

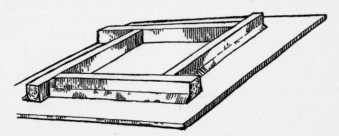

FIG. 39.—Slab to Receive Liquid Plaster.

that these shapes are pleasant and well harmonised with one another, and that the colour is good. Let each colour be bounded by the raised line so that no colour impinges upon another. Having drawn the design it may be traced through to the slab of plaster prepared for it. This slab is made by pouring liquid plaster into the space between four strips of wood arranged as shown in Fig. 39 on a sheet of glass. Needless to say, the space enclosed is 6¼ inches square. Glass is advised as it gives a delightfully smooth surface to the plaster, making it easy to work on. If the strips of wood are smooth and true they will lie in close contact with the glass, but to keep them in place when the weight of the plaster is pressing outwards, smear some soft clay into the outer angle between the wood and the glass, and also between the two strips of wood.

Mixing Plaster.—Into a clean bowl pour sufficient water for your purpose, and sprinkle the plaster into this, by allowing it to trickle between the fingers. When the plaster appears evenly just below the surface of the water stir briskly with a side-to-side motion until the mixture is of the consistency of thick cream.

Pour this into the space between the strips of wood and allow a quarter of an hour or so to set. Knock off the strips and remove the slab from the glass. It will be found that the under-side (in contact with the glass) is perfectly smooth. Upon this smooth surface place the design and trace through with a steel, or other hard point. The soft plaster readily takes an impression and the outline will be incised upon the plaster. With a fairly broad point (a boxwood tool cut to the required shape and size, and smoothed with fine glass-paper, or a stout wire filed to shape, are useful) scrape the lines to the required depth. Needless to say this is the mould, so that unless our design is symmetrical it must be reversed. Tiles which are not symmetrical, or are affected by being reversed, will need to be changed before being incised in the plaster. A tracing (on ordinary tracing paper) will serve this purpose. Into this mould the clay is pressed, after which it is fired and the glazes applied by hand ; unless the design is for one colour when it is merely " dipped." The illustrations show the mould (Plate XXII. (d)), an unglazed tile with its scheme of raised lines (Plate XXII. (e)), and the finished tile arranged both as a " side by side " and a " brickwise " repeat. This particular tile was designed for repetition in both ways (Plate XXIII. (b) and (d)). Another method of making the raised line tile is to apply " slip " (clay thinned with water until it flows easily) by means of a special syringe known as a " Squeegee," but this method hardly comes within the scope of this book.

MAJOLICA OR EMBOSSED TILES.

These tiles depend for their effect upon the soft gradations of colour, caused by the varied thickness of the glaze which spreads thinly over the raised portions and accumulates in the depressions. This should be borne in mind when preparing the design, and the relief planned accordingly. Prepare a design on paper with due regard for purpose, position, and method of repeat, allowing also for shrinkage. It is better to set out three or four squares of $6\frac{1}{4}$ inch sides and sketch the main lines in each one to ensure correct repetition. When the drawing is ready, prepare a slab of clay. Lay the drawing upon it and trace through with a hard point. The slab should be perfectly smooth as the modelling needs to be delicate, and the slightest projection from the ground easily apparent. The best way to prepare the slab is to nail four strips of wood 1 inch to $1\frac{1}{2}$ inches square to a board so that they enclose a space $6\frac{1}{4}$ inches square (Fig. 39). Into this space, press some clay (first rolling it between the palms) until it is level with the strips of wood. Strike off the superfluous clay with a straight-edge and fill in any cavities that may exist. Smooth again with the straight-edge, which, resting upon the strips of wood, will enable you to get the clay quite level.

Modelling.—Having traced the design through to this slab, place it in a strong side light and proceed with the modelling. Keep this as delicate as you can, and remember that the relief is enhanced by the glaze in the finished tile. When you have carried the modelling as far as you can, take a mould in plaster.

Moulding.—First arrange a raised border to contain the plaster, either of wood as described earlier, or clay bands. Mix the plaster and pour over the modelling to a thickness of 1 inch or so. Allow a quarter of an hour for it to set and then remove. A good deal of work can be done in the mould. Place the modelling and mould side by side and accustom yourself to seeing the relief in the clay, represented by a depression in the plaster. It follows that the work added in the mould will be raised in the finished tile, as you can only scrape away. It is possible, however, to add a good deal of sharpness and sparkle to the modelling by judicious work in the mould. The next stage is a cast from this mould, which may further be worked upon, as much may easily be done in the harder plaster which was difficult in the more yielding clay. The mould must be prepared before the plaster is poured into it, or the two may stick and refuse to come apart. Soak the mould in water until it has absorbed all it can, and then sponge over with soda-water (a large handful of common soda dissolved in a bucket of water) ; swill again and it is ready. Build a frame of clay or wood around the mould to keep the plaster in place, mix your plaster (as before) and fill up to a depth of 1 inch or so, taking care that the mould is still wet.

Separating.—When set the tile and mould must be separated. Place them in the sink and allow them to soak, then gently prise them apart. Don't hurry, but let the water soak well in before attempting to part them. Add any detail that may now be desirable, after which a final mould is taken. If necessary this mould may be worked upon as before. To see the progress of work in the mould a clay " squeeze " is taken by pressing clay into the mould, which upon removal gives an exact impression of the relief. The final mould is used for the finished tile, clay being pressed into it, and then fired and " dipped " in glaze. Should more than one colour be required the glazes are applied by hand. The illustrations show the mould (Plate XXII. (g)), a cast from it (Plate XXII. (f)), and the finished tile, arranged as a " side by side " repeat and also " brickwise " (Plate XXIII. (a) and (c)). There are other types of tile, but as they hardly come within the scope of this book, a very brief description will suffice :—

Painted tiles, sometimes painted in coloured glazes, and sometimes in under-glaze colours, and afterwards dipped in transparent glaze.

Printed tiles, a cheap process, where the pattern is transferred to the " biscuit " by means of transfer paper printed from an engraved copper plate.

Stencil plates are used for tiles and rich effects are obtainable.

Päte sur Päte is a white or coloured " slip " (clay thinned with water) applied to a ground of different colour. The colours are obtained by using metallic oxides, well ground and mixed with the clay. The " slip " is applied with a brush in successive layers, after which it may be worked with gravers and steel tools, when it has become fairly hard, by which means almost any degree of sharpness and finish is obtainable. The " slip " appears very opaque when first applied, but is rendered semi-transparent in the process of firing. The student is advised to bear this fact in mind when applying the " slip," as the ground colour affects the tint of the thin layers, but has little or no influence upon the thicker ones.

Encaustic tiles may be termed inlays, for the pattern is stamped or cut in the plastic clay of the tile, and into the cavities thus formed coloured " slips " are poured. When hard the surface is levelled by scraping with a steel tool. These tiles are useful for pavements, hearths, etc., as the depth of the pattern is calculated to stand hard wear. It is obvious from the above brief outline of the process that good, simple shapes form the most suitable designs for encaustic tiles. The " slips " must, of course, be made of the same clay throughout to ensure even shrinkage.

PLATE XXII.

(a)

(b)

(c)

(d)

(f)

(e)

(g)

(a), (b), (c). LETTERING.　　　(d), (e), (f), (g). TILE MODELLING. DE CLOISSONÉ LOW RELIEF.

PLATE XXIII.

(c)

(d)

(a)

(b)

FINISHED TILES.

CHAPTER XVIII.

STONE AND MARBLE CARVING.

"Sculpture" (Vasari tells us) " is an art which by removing all that is super-fluous from the material under treatment, reduces it to that form designed in the artist's mind." It is the reverse of modelling in that we start with a block larger than the finished work is to be, cutting away the stone until we arrive at the desired form. In modelling we start with a lump of clay much smaller than the ultimate work, and keep adding until we have built up the forms we need. The student is advised to start with a fairly soft stone and to acquire some familiarity with chisels and gouges and the way they work on the softer stone before attempting to cut marble. Caen stone, which is soft and cuts easily, at the same time allowing a fair degree of finish, is a very good stone to start with. A rigid stand is necessary to work upon, the stand used by the stone mason and known as a "banker" is specially adapted to carving, but any stand of suitable height, and rigid, will serve. The stone, unless of sufficient weight to stand firm, should be embedded in plaster or fixed in some way, so that it withstands the blows of the mallet. Having chosen a cast, or other suitable subject to copy, sketch the main lines and shapes on the stone, and proceed vigorously to rough out the chief masses. Study the work (and the copy) from all points of view, and watch the " planes " carefully.

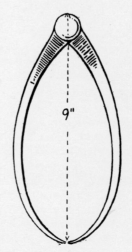

FIG. 40.—Callipers.

"**Roughing Out.**"—For roughing out, large tools should be used and struck firmly and strongly with the mallet. When the forms begin to approach those in the original the callipers (Fig. 40 shows a useful pair) should be used to test them. If the carving is larger or smaller than the original a scale may be used as described in " Modelling the Figure." This may seem unnecessary in a work that is being under-taken merely to learn the use of tools and materials, but it is advisable to start in the proper way, and to make a habit of doing everything as though it were an important commission.

Finishing.—As the stone approaches the final form smaller gouges will be used, and they should be driven in the directions of the sweeps and curves in the ornament. It should not be necessary to scrape and worry the stone into shape as it detracts from its interest. The tool marks in a good carving form a part of its charm, and certainly add to the vitality of the surface. It is essential that the tools should be kept sharp by rubbing them constantly on a piece of

York stone moistened with water.   The work of the Gothic carvers will provide
the student with fine examples for study in this type of work.   The management
of the light and shade, and vigorous treatment of relief ; the suitability of the
decoration to tools and material are well worthy of careful consideration.

MARBLE CARVING.

Marbles.—There are numerous types of marble, but only those known as
statuary marbles need be considered here.   Parian, Sicilian, Carrara, Pentelic,
and Serravezza are perhaps the best known of these.

Pentelic was used in the Parthenon, Erectheion, Thesion, and other Greek
sculptures.   It is obtained from Mount Pentelicus, near Athens, is harder to
work than Italian marble, but is more durable and weathers to a pleasant creamy
colour.   The Elgin marbles prove the durability of Pentelic stone.

Carrara was extensively used by the Romans under the name of Luna or
Luni.   During the Renaissance much of the marble used by the great Italian
sculptors came from these quarries.   Michelangelo spent considerable periods
there selecting material for his sculpture.

Serravezza, obtained from Mount Altessimi in Italy, is one of the best of
the statuary marbles.   At these quarries, again, Michelangelo spent some time
getting his material.

Parian comes from Mount Marpessa in the island of Paros, and is similar to
Pentelic.

Sicilian is a hard material, but rather opaque in appearance and more suitable for outdoor work than for statuary.

Before attempting an important work in marble, it is necessary to prepare
a full-size model in clay ; for in this material faults detected may easily be recti-
fied by adding, cutting away, or even bending a limb, or torso, if necessary.
The armature being constructed of lead piping admits of considerable alterations
in pose without destroying the modelling of the figure.   Such alterations being
impossible in the rigid marble it is essential that pose and modelling should be
carefully thought out first in the more plastic clay.   It is then converted into
plaster, and is ready for its final translation into marble.   If we start straight
away on the marble, with no preliminary model, there is every possibility of
some error in pose or proportion which will ruin the whole work.   The Greeks
during their finest period attacked the marble with no preliminary preparation
save a small sketch.   This method seems to have obtained until fairly late in
the first century B.C., when we read of Pasiteles, a painstaking sculptor, who
never executed a work without first modelling it.   The method employed prior
to this is described by Professor Ernest Gardner.   Having obtained a block of
marble of the required shape and size they commenced with a front view, and
hewed away the marble at the two sides until the correct contour had been obtained.   Turning to the side of the block they next worked in a similar manner
on the front and back contours until these too resembled the lines required.
The block now, if regarded from the front, back, or sides, would resemble the
desired figure, but the section would be square.   The next stage therefore was
to round the figure and to introduce the surface modelling.   A small sketch
model and a system of measurement may be taken for granted, but " pointing "
as we understand it was probably unknown.   From Cellini and Vasari we may

gather some idea of the methods used by the sculptors of the Italian Renaissance. Vasari in his " Life of Michael Angelo " tells us that " David," the
colossal marble statue, was carved with the sole aid of a small wax model.
Cellini says that " Michael Angelo, who had experience of both methods, that
is to say, of carving statues, alike from the small model and the big, and at the
end, convinced of their respective advantages and disadvantages, adopted the
second method (of the full-sized model). And this I saw myself at Florence
when he was working in the sacristy of S. Lorenzo (on the Medici tombs)."
Donatello, we learn from the same source, used the small model, as did many
other " ' excellent masters,' boldly attacking the marble with their tools, as
soon as they had carved the little model to completion, yet at the end they have
found themselves but little satisfied with their work." The Greek carver had
a wonderfully intimate knowledge of his material, combined with a clear conception of the desired result. Michelangelo, though a master of the technique
of carving, sometimes made mistakes in his calculations, the " Slave " in the
Louvre has not been allowed sufficient marble for the leg. Lacking as we do
the tradition and practice of the ancients, it is safer for us to make a full-size
model before commencing work on the marble. There are undoubtedly men
to-day who dispense with it, and who work direct in marble, but they are
very few, and the method is not a safe one for the student. Having prepared
the model and converted it into plaster it becomes necessary to choose the
marble. This is rather a delicate business, and it is better to enlist the aid of an
expert until such time as we have acquired some skill ourselves. There are
two tests, however, which may be employed in judging the quality of the marble.
By pouring water over the block any veins or specks that may exist (even when
below the surface) will become visible. Again, if the marble upon being struck
with an iron hammer emits a clear, ringing note, it is less likely to possess
flaws or vents than when the note is cracked and dull. Having chosen the
block and transported it to the studio it is placed in position on the banker, with
the plaster model arranged conveniently alongside.

Pointing.—The next stage is the " pointing." For this process a pointing
machine (Fig. 41) is required. This machine is simply a contrivance for transferring measurements from the plaster to the marble. It is composed of a rod
with three fixed points, and one movable point. The three fixed points must
have three corresponding spots arranged on the plaster and on the marble so
that the machine may be fixed into the same position for each measurement
taken with the movable point. The spots, in marble and plaster, are marked
by copper rivets with a shallow depression (to receive the points) drilled in the
head of each, the rivets being embedded in plaster, which when set will keep
them in position as long as they are required. The pointing machine is first
placed in position on the plaster, with its three points resting in the hollows at
the head of the copper rivets, and the movable needle (working on a ball and
socket joint) placed into position on the highest projection on the cast. When
the position is settled the needle is fixed by means of thumbscrews. The
machine is now transferred to the marble, the three points being again set upon
the corresponding copper rivets. It will now be found that the pointing needle
cannot be pressed home until some of the material has been chipped away.
When a certain amount has been cleared, leaving plenty for future stages, a
drill is employed and a hole drilled until the needle reaches almost to the required
depth. It is dangerous to force the needle quite " home," for all the measure-

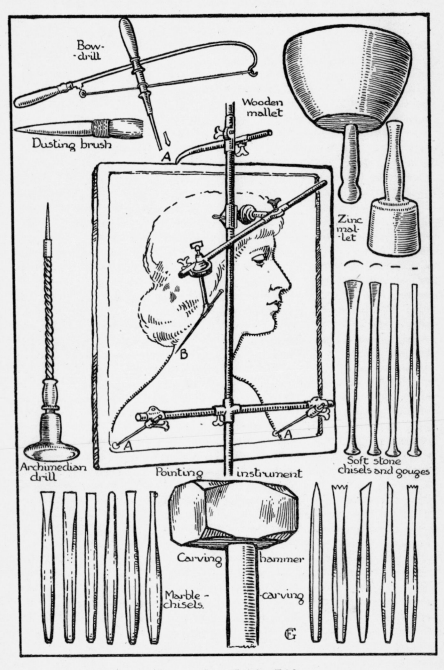

FIG. 41.—Stone Carving Tools.

ments must be kept "full," say from a 32nd to a 16th of an inch from the ultimate depth. This allows sufficient material for finishing and surface modelling.
A series of points are found in a similar manner fairly close together on important surfaces, and farther apart on broad planes of drapery or less important
parts. Each point is first taken on the model, and then carefully transferred
to the marble into which the drill is inserted, until the needle may be pressed to
within a fraction of the full measurement. When all the necessary points
have been found, the surface of the marble will be pitted with drill holes, with
intervening mounds of material which need clearing away.

Finishing.—After this superfluous marble has been chipped away to the
level of the drill holes, the work will begin to resemble the model. The next,
and final, stage is one that requires care and skill. It is quite usual for the
sculptor to employ a workman to "point" his marble, but at this stage he
takes the work in hand himself, for now the surface modelling, textures, and
refinements of chiselling must come into play. It is now the work of the
sculptor himself, he alone can produce just the effect, the particular degree of
finish he desires. The workman, if skilful, could doubtless produce a good copy
of the plaster model, but it would probably be mechanical, lacking in individuality. Marble, especially the bust statuary, is more transparent than plaster,
or flesh, and the darks have therefore a tendency to become lighter when translated. This is particularly noticeable in the nostrils, where the wings of the
nose, if made too thin, will allow the light to penetrate, and so tend to destroy
the darks which exist in the more opaque plaster or flesh. It requires some
study, and also practice, to appreciate the correct treatment needed for the
various parts of the work.

Use of Tools.—The tools, when cutting, should be held at a fairly acute
angle to the surface of the marble, just sufficient to bite into it and remove small
chips. It is a mistake to hold the tools near the vertical, or to attempt to chip
off large pieces. It is safer to take off too little than too much, for it is always
possible to take more off, but once off it cannot be replaced. The tools used for
finishing should be finer than those used for roughing out, or for the intermediate
stage; see that they are kept sharp at all stages. The hammers also might be
varied, using a fairly heavy one of about 4 lb. for clearing away the stuff between
the points, a lighter one of about 3 lb. for the intermediate stage, and a light
one of about 2 lb. for the delicate surface modelling. Round-nosed drills are
useful for such hollows as the gouges or chisels will not enter easily. Rifflers
and files are also useful on occasion, but should at all times be used sparingly.
Finishing should be proceeded with slowly and thoughtfully, as upon the
treatment now given to the work much of its value will depend. The degree
of finish to be given to each portion, whether it should be smoothed with
files and rifflers or even sandpaper, or whether it would be better left with
the chisel marks upon it will depend upon the texture needed, and the taste
and skill of the sculptor. Fig. 41 shows the principal tools required for stone
carving.

CHAPTER XIX.

METAL CASTING.

As metal can only be cast in a molten condition, the mould must necessarily be of some material sufficiently impervious to heat, and at the same time plastic enough to take a clear impression. The materials most common are: plaster of Paris and powdered brick, metal, for casting others more easily fused, and sand, the last being the most frequently employed. For sand

FIG. 42.—Section of Sand Mould.

casting, where the model is not too complicated, say some such section as shown in Fig. 42, the procedure is fairly straightforward.

Flasks.—Take two iron frames large enough to receive the model and to allow for the pour; this should be sufficiently far away to give a good weight of metal above, which will force the molten material into all parts of the mould (Fig. 43). These frames, called flasks, are rectangular, from 2 to 3 inches deep, the upper one having four pins which fit into four corresponding rings in the lower one. This is to enable the two flasks to be placed into correct relationship with each other (see Fig. 43). The lower half of the flask is laid upon a board just large enough to project slightly beyond the frame, and rammed full of casting sand.

Sand.—This sand is really a mixture of fine sand and loam, pure sand being too loose to bind together, the necessary adhesive quality being supplied by the

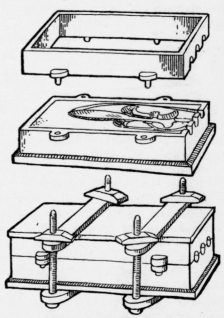

FIG. 43.—Iron Moulding Frames.

loam. The proportions of each will depend somewhat upon the metal to be cast and the quality of the work, but always as little loam should be used as will serve to bind the mould. Having filled the lower frame with damp sand

and loam, and well rammed it in with a mallet, level the upper surface with a straight-edge. Over this surface sprinkle evenly a couple of handfuls of sand, lay a board upon it and strike sharply and evenly with the mallet. This helps to consolidate the sand. Remove the board and once more strike off the super-fluous sand with the straight-edge. Lay the model in position, not too near the pouring holes, and not too far away (Fig. 44). For, as previously stated, if the model is too near the pour the weight of metal will not be sufficient to force itself into the interstices, whereas if too far away there is a risk of its cooling on the journey. Having settled the position of the model, scoop out a hollow corresponding to the depth of one half of the pattern and press it well home. Dust it over first of all with French chalk or blacklead, to ensure it leaving the mould clearly.

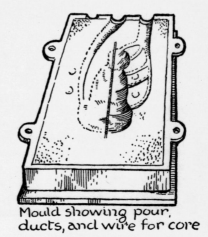

Mould showing pour, ducts, and wire for core

FIG. 44.

Preparation of Pattern.—The model or pattern, whether of wood or plaster, should be allowed to dry thoroughly and then given a coating of shellac, otherwise there is a danger of the sand adhering to it. The French chalk or blacklead is merely a further safeguard, although the smooth shiny surface so obtained will also give a better impression in the mould, and consequently a sharper casting. Having pressed the pattern well into the lower flask the whole surface should be dusted over with red brick-dust, the superfluous dust being brushed off with a soft camel-hair mop, after which the loose particles are blown away.

Upper Frame.—The upper frame is now fitted into place, *i.e.* the pins are dropped into the corresponding rings in the lower one. Carefully press fine sand well over the model to ensure that all the interstices are filled, and then ram the frame full of sand. Level this off, sprinkle over a little extra, after-wards laying the board on top and striking with the mallet as before. Strike off with straight edge again, replace board, and separate the two halves. Take out the model and scoop a channel from the cavity to be filled to the pouring hole in the flask. This, of course, must be done in both halves of the mould. It is usually better to carry the channel down to the base of the mould, so that the metal entering below will gradually rise and fill the mould (Fig. 44). There is a danger, when the metal enters from above, that the force of its downward rush will carry away such portions of the mould as happen to project. When the pour has been arranged, it will be necessary to cut a few vents for the escape of air, which would otherwise be imprisoned and might cause an explosion.

Treating the Surface.—The face of the mould receiving the metal is now dusted over with meal-dust or waste flour, or, for fine work, charcoal, loamstone, or rotten stone. For gold or silver casting, the smoke from a lighted torch or taper is often used. The smooth, sooty deposit so obtained gives a good surface. Having completed the pour, and vents, and prepared the surface, fit the frames together again, replace the boards at top and bottom, and fix securely with screw clamps (see Fig. 43). The mould now requires drying and the greater the proportion of loam there is, the more necessary it is to thoroughly dry it. It has been said that the proportions of sand and loam depend to some extent upon the nature and quality of the work in hand. If the mixture is damp with a large proportion of loam it will ram more tightly into the mould and will take a better impression of the model with less likelihood of crumbling. But, on the other hand, the close, impervious nature of this material is more liable to accident when the metal is poured, owing to damp and the non-escape of hot air. Again, when the casting cools it contracts slightly, and should the mould be too hard to give with the cooling metal, cracks are likely to occur in the latter. If such a mould is used it is, therefore, essential to dry thoroughly, but it is far safer to keep the sand as dry as possible, and to use as little loam as will serve to bind. Moulds for copper, bronze and brass need to be drier than those used for iron. When thoroughly dry the flask is placed in an almost vertical position and the metal poured in from the crucible. The foregoing brief description will explain the process of casting simple objects which are not " undercut " and will " draw " easily from the mould, the latter being in two sections only.

PIECE MOULDING.

Where the model is undercut or in any way complicated it will be necessary to make the mould in separate pieces to allow the model to be withdrawn

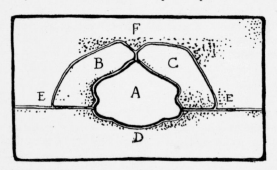

FIG. 45.—Section of Model.

without damaging the sand in which it is invested. The impression left must be clean and true or the casting will be poor. Let us suppose that the section of the model is similar to that shown in Fig. 45 A. It is obvious that when embedded in sand, it would lift easily enough from the lower mould D, but owing to undercutting the upper half, BC, if made in one piece, would not lift off cleanly. This upper portion has consequently to be made in two pieces, B, C. The procedure is as follows: The model will probably be in plaster of Paris, which has been allowed to dry and coated with shellac. Take a pair of flasks; place the lower one on a board, large enough to project beyond the flask, and fill up with casting sand. The flasks should be large enough to take the model and to allow sufficient room for the pour. Ram the sand well in with the mallet, level the upper surface with a straight-edge, sprinkle a little more sand over the top and replace the board. Strike the board sharply and evenly with the mallet to drive the sand well home, and to produce a compact, homogeneous mass. Remove the board and level with the straight-edge. Upon this surface lay the model face upwards. Take care to place it far enough from the pouring hole for reasons previously stated.

Moulding.—When the position of the model has been settled, excavate a hollow in the sand just large enough to take the lower portion of the cast D (Fig. 45). Lay the model in position in this cavity and fill in with fine sand until the whole is well supported (having first brushed the model over with French chalk or blacklead). Dust over with fine brick-dust, and with a fine camel-hair mop brush well over the whole surface, finally blowing away the superfluous dust. The next procedure is to make the two separate pieces B, C. Dust the pattern again with French chalk or blacklead, blowing away the surplus. Take some of the sand and press it carefully into the hollows, after which build it up until it assumes the section shown in C. Tap this evenly with the mallet to consolidate it, and to drive it into close contact with the model. True up the edge of the seam F with a modelling tool or steel spatula, and smooth up the outer surface until it is true and even. This piece should now be lifted off and dusted with finely powdered charcoal. First tap the lower board until you see that you have loosened the piece, and then with the aid of a couple of stout iron wires, sharpened to a point inserted into a wooden handle (Fig. 46), raise the piece. After dusting with charcoal, replace in position. The piece on the opposite side, D, is now made in exactly the same manner. It now remains to fill the upper flask with sand, to hold these pieces in place. First dust the whole surface of the pieces and the under mould BCE over with brick-dust, lay the upper flask in position and fill up with sand rammed well in with the mallet. Strike off level with the straight-edge, adding a few more handfuls, tapping the upper board and again striking off as before. Carefully reverse the flask and lift off the under frame. This will discover the two pieces and the model lying in

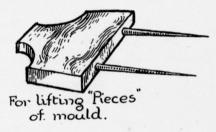

For lifting "Pieces" of mould.

FIG. 46.

position in the upper frame. Hollow out two circular depressions, with the end of a modelling tool or spatula, in the flat surfaces of each of the two pieces (where they come into contact with the lower mould). These will give rise to corresponding projections in the under mould, and will act as keys to ensure placing them in their correct positions. The mould in the lower frame was merely a temporary one, serving to hold the pattern whilst constructing the front portion. Knock the sand out of this lower frame and replace on the upper one. Dust over the surface of the mould with brick-dust, and carefully press the sand over the back of the model, finally filling the flask with sand, levelling, driving home with the mallet, and replacing the board as before. Separate the mould, take out the model, replace the pieces and arrange the pour (gates if necessary) and the vents for the escape of hot air. The pour is a funnel-shaped channel, widest where the metal enters; the gates are minor channels arranged to enter the mould at various projecting points (Fig. 44), and leading out of the main channel or pour. It is usually better, as stated before, to let the metal enter the mould at or near the base and fill up gradually, as the rush of metal downwards is apt to sweep away delicate projections. Press the sand well together round the mouth of the pour with the thumb, lest it should crumble under the pressure of the incoming metal. Vents should also be made from projecting portions to allow the hot air to escape, although where the sand is fairly loose and the work small this is not always necessary. It is as well, however, to take every precaution against accidents, as they are not only apt to spoil the casting but are also liable to cause injury to the incautious caster. Having scooped the channels for pour, gates, and vents in both sides of the mould fit the two frames together and fix firmly with screw clamps. Dry thoroughly and the mould is now ready for the metal. This, however, is assuming that the cast required is a solid one ; should a hollow cast be desired it will be necessary to make a core. The core is made of sand and loam (occasionally horse dung is mixed with it, which, being afterwards burned, leaves the core very porous) and is placed in the centre of the mould with a space between it and the walls of the mould equivalent to the thickness of metal required. It is obvious that the core will need support or it will fall against the mould. An iron wire is therefore laid lengthwise in the cavity supported by the sand at top and bottom. In order to give the sand a better grip, a thin copper wire is wound tightly round and then smeared with thick paste. The mould being opened and the pattern removed, this wire is laid in position, and

The Core

FIG. 47.

the front half of the mould (Fig. 44) filled tightly with the sand and loam. This gives an exact reproduction of the front half of the model. More sand is now pressed on to this as nearly as possible of the same bulk and shape as the back portion of the model. Press the lower frame (containing the mould of the back) on to this, and so obtain a complete replica of the pattern in sand with the wire passing through the centre (Fig. 47). This will form the core, but as it fits exactly to the inside of the mould it is evident that no metal could penetrate. It is therefore necessary to pare away the outer portion of the core to a depth of from rather less than $\frac{1}{8}$-inch for silver to about $\frac{3}{16}$-inch for brass or bronze. The space thus left between core and outer mould will be filled with metal the thickness of which will be equivalent to the amount pared away. The core is sometimes burned before paring, and sometimes pared in the green state. Replace the core in the mould, supported at either end by the projecting wire (Fig. 47), fit the flasks together with the boards above and below, fix with screw clamps, dry and pour as before.

CASTING A RELIEF IN METAL.

Relief modellings, such as a portrait in low relief, may be cast as follows : A cast is taken in plaster (Fig. 48) which is dried and coated with shellac. When this has hardened some blacklead or French chalk is brushed over, which ensures a smooth surface and facilitates removal from the sand. An empty flask is now placed about this cast as it lies on a board (the flask framing the cast as it were). See that the cast is sufficiently far from the pouring hole for reasons previously stated. Carefully press fine casting sand over the surface of the cast, finally filling the flask with sand. Level off with a straight-edge add a little more sand, place a board on the top and strike evenly with the mallet to press the mould well together. Level off again and remove the mould

from the cast. We have now a reversed replica (or mould) of the relief modelling (Fig. 48). Roll out a thin sheet of clay, even and smooth in texture, to the
same thickness as you desire your casting to be. Press this gently and evenly
into the mould, for upon this clay will depend the thickness of your metal (Fig.
48). Place the lower half of the flask
in position, after dusting the first with
charcoal dust. Ram this flask full of
sand, level as before, and lift away
(Fig. 48). The clay is now carefully
taken off, leaving a space between the
two moulds to be occupied later by
metal. Grooves or ingates are scooped
from the pouring hole to the mould,
also vents; and the surface dusted
over with charcoal and rotten stone
mixed. The whole is well dried and
the surface smoked with a torch or
taper, or by holding over a fire of cork
shavings. After which the frames are

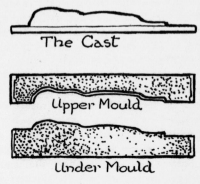

FIG. 48.

screwed together and the metal poured. Another method, similar to the
waste-wax process is to make a plaster mould of the relief, dry, and coat with
shellac. A coating of wax, corresponding in thickness to the metal casting,
is given to the mould, and this coating or shell of wax when thoroughly
hardened is removed and moulded in sand in the same way as the last
(Fig. 48).

FIGURE CASTING. WASTE-WAX.

For figure casting the sand process is a very complicated one, as may easily
be imagined when we remember that the mould must be so constructed that
each portion must leave the work or " draw " without hindrance. The student
familiar with " Piece Moulding " in plaster will readily understand this. A good
look at a plaster figure as it leaves the caster's hands with the seams visible will
help us to realise what a multitude of pieces are necessary for even the simplest
figure. This method of reproduction has now been almost entirely superseded
by the " Waste-Wax " process, or by electrotyping, and so a description is
hardly necessary. The " Cire Perdu " or waste-wax process is pretty much the
same to-day as it was in the time of Benvenuto Cellini, as may easily be seen in
the extracts given here. A plaster cast is prepared by the modeller, and from
this a piece mould or a gelatine mould is taken. Gelatine is rather better as it
leaves fewer seams for the sculptor to touch up. Molten wax is painted in
successive coats over the mould until a thickness equivalent to that desired for
the metal is obtained, for this wax when melted out will be replaced by bronze.
When the mould has been coated with wax to the required depth the portions
are fitted together and bound up securely. The advantage of this method is
that the thickness of the wax may be varied so that the bronze which will ultimately replace it, will be thicker where weight and strength are required, and
thinner where an extended limb or other portion requires lightness. The
cavity inside the wax has now to be filled with a mixture of plaster and
powdered brick (about one-third plaster to two of brick-dust) in a liquid state.

This is known as the core, and should the casting be large it will be necessary to fix iron supports inside.   When the core is set the outer mould is taken off, leaving a wax replica of the plaster figure, supported by the core inside.   The surface of the wax must now be remodelled at the seams and such other places as are necessary, after which small rods of bronze are inserted into the core through the wax and allowed to project somewhat beyond the figure.   These are to keep the core and the outer mould in their relative positions when the wax is melted out, and being bronze (the same metal as the casting), can be cut off and filed level without affecting the surface, when the figure is finished. The next stage is the arrangement of ducts for the outflow of the wax, and later the escape of the air replaced by the molten bronze, and also the "in-gates" through which the metal will enter the mould.   The ducts are so arranged as to allow such air to escape as would otherwise become trapped (perhaps causing an explosion).   For instance, if the bronze is poured into the base of a figure (and so by means of feet and legs to the other portions) and the arms are free of the body it will be necessary to fit ducts from the fingers, or the bronze rising in the arms will force the air upwards to the fingers, and failing an outlet, will explode, or, at the best, cause air-bubbles.   The ducts are formed by fixing rods of wax to such parts of the figure as occasion demands.   These, when melted out, will leave channels for the escape of air.   The ingates are also rods of wax, and need very careful consideration when fixing.   It is some-times better to carry the bronze to the bottom of the mould (outside) before allowing it to enter the figure.   It rises gradually and forces the air upwards through the ducts until the top is reached.   Under these conditions the ingate must be so arranged as to carry the bronze to the base of the mould before. allowing it to enter.   When ducts and ingates are settled the mould has to be made.   A fine coating of clay, powdered brick, and plaster is carefully brushed over the wax model to exclude air-bubbles and to ensure a good coating over the whole work.   This first coat must be of fine texture, the succeeding ones may be coarser, but sufficient should be laid on to give a good strong shell. The projecting ends of the bronze rods will be embedded in this shell, whilst the other ends are embedded in the core, the centre portions lying in the wax.

Melting out the Wax.—This wax has now to be melted out.   The whole is placed in the casting pit and heated until the wax runs from the mould. A certain proportion will be absorbed by the core and the outer shell, and will help to strengthen them.   An expert caster can gauge the quantity that should flow out, and can thus tell when the mould is empty.   The mould is thoroughly annealed (heated and allowed to cool).   It is then built up with sand, care being taken to bring all the air ducts to the surface and to see that none are choked, and the bronze poured in.   When cool the mould is removed, the core raked out, and all projections, rods, ducts, etc., sawn and filed off, when the statue is complete.

CELLINI'S METHOD OF CASTING.

Benvenuto Cellini's "Autobiography" gives an interesting account of the methods he employed when casting the "Perseus," modelled by him for Duke Cosimo de Medici.   I can hardly do better than transcribe as far as possible Benvenuto's own inimitable description.   The Duke had commissioned him to make a model of Perseus.   "So," says he, "I set to the task with great goodwill, and in a few weeks I had finished it. It was made of yellow wax about a cubit in height and very delicately wrought, for I had given all my best skill and knowledge to the making of it." Here follows a grumble at the negligence of the Duke who kept him waiting several days before taking the trouble to look at his model. When he did set eyes upon it, however, " he was so pleased, and praised it so extravagantly that I had good hope of having found in him a patron of some discrimination. He examined it for a long time with ever-growing delight, and then he said, ' Benvenuto, my friend, if you can carry out this little model on a large scale it will be the finest thing in the Piazza.'" Benvenuto, with a touch of modesty unusual for him, replied, "My most excellent lord, in the Piazza are works by the great Donatello and the marvellous Michel-angelo, the two greatest men since the ancients. Nevertheless, as your most illustrious Excellency is so encouraging to my model, I feel within me the power to do the complete work three times as well." This is more characteristic of our author, and he continues in similar style. " These works of mine stirred up a deal of argument; for the Duke kept saying that he understood such things perfectly, and knew just what could be done. I replied that my work would decide this dispute and his doubt, though most certainly I should achieve more for his Excellency than I had promised him." He continues in this vein for some pages, varying his boasting by abusing those who would thwart him, especially one Baccio Bandinelli. He never allows an opportunity for venting his spleen on Baccio to escape him, for his hatred of this rival was whole-hearted and deep. He then returns to " Perseus," or rather to the " Medusa." " That woman writhing under the feet of Perseus. The casting was a matter of the utmost difficulty, and to avoid any mistake I determined to use all the knowledge I had been at such pains to acquire. Thus the first cast I made in my little furnace was perfectly successful; and so clean was it that my friends thought there was no need for me to touch it up again. Of course, certain Germans and Frenchmen who plume themselves on knowing wonderful secrets, declare they can cast bronze so that it needs no retouching; but this is foolish talk, for after bronze has been cast it must be worked on with hammer and chisels in the fashion of the marvellous antique masters, and of the moderns too; at least, such moderns as have learnt anything at all about the matter." For some sixteen pages he leaves " Perseus " to detail other activities, to give his version of a violent quarrel with Bandinelli, and to grumble about the Duke who certainly treated him somewhat cavalierly, if what he says is true. He then returns to his casting. " I had cast the ' Medusa,' and it had come out per-fectly; so I had great hopes of doing as well with my ' Perseus.' The wax had been worked over it and I assured myself that in bronze it would be just as successful as the ' Medusa.' In wax the thing looked so fine that the Duke was much pleased with its beauty. But either some one had made him believe that it would fail in bronze, or he imagined this of himself; at all events one day, when he had come to see me, which he did with uncommon frequency at that time, he said to me, ' Benvenuto, the statue cannot be a success in bronze for the rules of the art do not permit of it.' I felt the words of his Excellency very keenly, and I replied, ' My lord, I know you have little faith in me, and this I believe is due to your having too much faith in those who speak ill of me, or because you know nothing of the matter.' He hardly let me finish ere he cut in : ' I profess to know a great deal; and what is more, I do know what I am talking about.' Whereupon I replied, ' Yes, like a prince; not as an artist.

For did your Excellency understand the matter as you think you do, you would believe me on the strength of the great bronze bust I made of you which was sent to Elba, . . . likewise the casting of the ' Medusa,' which your Excellency sees now before you—and a difficult casting it was, such as no other man had ever done before me in this devilish art.' " We must assume that Benvenuto has lost his temper to speak so rudely to a Duke. " Look, my lord ! I made that furnace over again on a different system from any other ; for besides the new improvements and clever inventions to be seen in it I made two issues for the bronze ; otherwise this difficult contorted figure could never have come out so successfully. It is all due to my intelligence that it did not fail, and that I carried through what none of the masters of the art believed possible. Know also, my lord, that of a truth with all the great and complicated works I did in France under that marvellous King Francis, I succeeded admirably ; and this only because of the encouragement which the good King gave me by his handsome provision for my needs, and his grant of as many workmen as I asked for. Indeed there were times when I employed more than forty, all chosen by myself. That was the reason I did so many fine things in so short a time." " So there, now," one can imagine him concluding, but he continues in this strain for a greater length than our space will allow us to follow him, then back once more to his casting. " I set about procuring several loads of pine from the pine woods of Serrestori, near Monte Lupo ; while I was waiting for these, I covered my ' Perseus ' with the clay I had got ready several months before in order that it might be well seasoned. When I had made the ' tunic ' of clay—for so it is called in our art—and had most carefully armed and girt it with iron, I began to draw off the wax by a slow fire through the various vent-holes I had made ; the more of these you have the better will your mould fill." This was the mould and out of it he melts the wax of which the figure was modelled. In speaking of the " Medusa " he describes his methods of construction in that case, so, as he says nothing about this part of " Perseus," we must assume he adopted the same process for both figures. " There I began the figure of ' Medusa.' First I made a framework of iron, then covered it with clay ; and when that was done I baked it." In another place he says he made this figure " about half an inch thinner than the finished figure was to be . . . and spread wax on the top, modelling this with the utmost care." Presumably the wax was half an inch thick to bring the figure to its proper size. Returning to " Perseus." When this wax was melted from the mould he " built up round it a funnel-shaped furnace of bricks, arranged one above the other, so as to leave numerous openings for the fire to breathe through. Then, very gradually, I laid the wood on, and kept the fire for two days and two nights on end. After I had drawn off all the wax, and the mould had been properly baked, I set to work to build a hole to sink the thing in, attending to all the strictest rules of the great art. This done I raised the mould with the utmost care by means of windlasses and strong ropes to an upright position, and suspended it a cubit above the level of the furnace ; sparing no pains to settle it securely there. This difficult job over, I set about propping it up with the earth I had dug out of the hole ; and as I built up the earth I made vent-holes, that is little pipes of terra-cotta such as are used for drains and things of that kind. Then I saw that it was quite firm, and that this way of banking it up and putting conduits in their proper places was likely to be successful. It was evident also that my workmen understood my mode of working which was very different from that of any other masters in my profession. Sure, therefore, that I could trust them, I gave my attention to the furnace, which I had filled up with pigs of copper and pieces of bronze, laid one on top of the other—according to the rules of the craft—that is, not pressing too closely one on the other, but arranged so that the flames could make their way freely about them ; for in this manner the metal is more quickly affected by the heat and liquefied. Then, in great excitement, I ordered them to light the furnace. They piled on the pine logs ; and between the unctuous pine resin and the well-con-trived draught of the furnace, the fire burned so splendidly that I had to feed it now on one side and now on the other. The effort was almost intolerable, yet I forced myself to keep it up. On top of all this the shop took fire, and we feared lest the roof should fall upon us. Then, too, from the garden, the rain and the wind blew in with such chill gusts as to cool the furnace. All this fighting for so many hours with adverse circumstances, forcing myself to a labour such as even my robust health could not stand, ended in a one-day fever of indescribable severity." So he goes to bed, after begging his men to do their utmost during his absence. Naturally his malady was of a terrible nature, far worse than any human being had ever suffered from before ; he tells them : " By to-morrow I shall be dead," and we must suppose he honestly thought so. But his remedy was a queer one, which could hardly be recommended in ordi-nary cases. Warned by a man " whose body was twisted like a capital S " that his work was ruined, he jumped out of bed and " dealt kicks and blows to the servant girls, the boy and everyone who came to help me, wailing the while, ' Ah, traitors ! jealous monsters ! this is a malicious plot. But I swear by God that I shall come at the truth of it, and before I die I will give to the world such proof of my strong hand as shall make more than one man stand and wonder.' " He hurries to the shop and finds his men dazed, and breaks into their stupor with : " Wake up ! Listen to me ! Since you've been either too great fools or too great knaves to do as I told you, attend to me now. I am here in front of my work. And not a word from any of you ; for it's help, not advice that will serve me now." One ventures to answer him but he turned on him with fury and with murder in his eye, and so completely cows him. " I hurried to the furnace," Benvenuto proceeds, " and found the metal had all coagulated, or, as we say, ' caked.' I ordered two labourers to go to Capretta, the butcher opposite, for a load of young oak logs which had been dry for more than a year, and which Madonna Genevra, Capretta's wife had already offered me. As soon as I got the first armfuls, I set about filling the ash-pit below the furnace. Now, oak of this kind makes a fiercer fire than any other sort of wood, and that is why alder or pine is used for the founding of gun-metal for which the fire should be slow. Ah ! then you should have seen how the cake of metal began to run and how it glowed. Meanwhile, too, I forced it to flow along the channels, while I sent the rest of the men on the roof to see after the fire which had broken out again more fiercely now the furnace was burning with such fury ; and towards the garden side I made them pile up planks and rugs and old hang-ings to prevent the rain from pouring in. When I had mastered all the confu-sion and trouble, I shouted now to this man, now to that, bidding them fetch and carry for me, and the solidified metal beginning to melt just then, the whole band were so excited to obedience that each man did the work of three. Then I bade them fetch half a pig of pewter, weighing about sixty pounds, and this I threw right into the middle of the furnace. And what with the wood I had put in beneath, and all the stirring with iron rods and bars, in a little while the mass grew liquid. When I saw I had raised the dead, in despite of all those ignorant sceptics, such vigour came back to me that the remembrance of my fever and the fear of death passed from me utterly. Then, suddenly we heard a great noise, and saw a brilliant flash of fire just as if a thunderbolt had rushed into our very midst." They were all dazed but discovered that the lid of the furnace had blown open so that the bronze was running over. " In an instant I had every mouth of the mould open and the plugs closed. But, perceiving that the metal did not run as freely as it should, I came to the conclusion that the intense heat had consumed all the alloy. So I bade them fetch every pewter dish and porringer and plate I had in the house, nearly two hundred in all, and part of them I threw, one after another into the channels, and put the rest into the furnace. Then they saw my bronze was really melted and filling up the mould, and gave me the readiest and most cheerful help and obedience." The mould full, Benvenuto betakes himself to bed. " For two days I let my work cool, and then uncovered a little bit at a time. First of all I found that, thanks to the vents, the head of ' Medusa ' had come out splendidly . . . the other head, that of ' Perseus,' was just as perfect ; at which I wondered more ; for, as you can see, it is much lower than that of ' Medusa.' I had placed the mouths of the mould above the head and on the shoulders of the ' Perseus,' and now I found that this head had taken all the remaining bronze in my furnace. Wonderful to relate there was nothing left in the mouth of the channel and yet there had been enough for my purpose." Clever Benvenuto !—sufficient to say that the whole cast came out successfully except the toes and a small portion of the right foot. But as this only proved a statement he had previously made when arguing with the Duke he is rather pleased than otherwise, despite the fact that it means extra work. This extract has been given at some length as there is a peculiar charm about Cellini's mode of relating his achievements, a charm that seemed worth preserving as far as possible. And allowing for possible exaggerations, and a magnifying of the difficulties he had to contend with, it was certainly no light labour to cast a figure in bronze when the whole work, from modelling the form, to constructing the furnace and melting and pouring the metal, was necessarily the work of one man. The student is advised to read this " Autobiography," a translation of which, by Anne Macdonell, is published in the " Everyman " series by Messrs. Dent.

It will be noted that the method of casting by the Cire-perdu or waste-wax process as here described is essentially the same as that in use to-day. Some further notes from " The Treatise on Sculpture," by Benvenuto, translated by C. R. Ashbee, may help to clear up any obscurities that may exist in the fore-going account. When casting a small figure you first model the figure, and then cover it with tin-foil, which is stuck on with paste or boiled turpentine ; oil it to prevent the gesso (plaster) from adhering ; and make a piece mould. Care should be exercised to ensure that each piece of the mould will " pull." Into each of these pieces is fitted a small loop of iron wire. The outer side of the pieces is oiled, and the loops embedded in clay to keep them from adhering to the matrix or outer mould. This is made in two pieces (front and back) and is intended to keep the small separate pieces in position. The mould is then allowed to dry (Cellini advises tying it together tightly to keep it from warping). Take the mould apart and fix each piece in its place in the matrix by means of the loop of iron wire which is tied by a strong cord passed through a hole in the

Plate XXIV.

Sculptures on the Façade of the Second Propylon of the Temple of Isis at Philæ, Egypt.

PLATE XXV.

(b) SEATED FIGURE OF QUEEN TETA-KHART (Egyptian, XVIIIth Dynasty).

(a) COLOSSAL FIGURE AT THE TEMPLE OF ABON SIMBEL, EGYPT. Note Figures in Relief on the Wall behind.

matrix to a splint of wood on the outside. Grease the mould with lard and lay on a coat of wax or clay. Fit inside an iron framework and mould clay over it (the clay is mixed with shavings of cloth and allowed to stand for three or four months to allow the fabric to decompose). Fill up the interior of the mould (inside the clay or wax) and allow to dry, after which it is bound with thin iron wire and fired. The clay or wax (which represents the bronze in the finished casting) is removed, the core being coated with a thin solution of powdered bone, brick-dust, and clay. The iron framework should be in actual contact with the mould in three or four places. This is instead of the rods of bronze used by modern casters, and is intended to keep the core in position when the wax (or clay) is removed. Make holes in the mould for inlets, or pours, fix the core in position, and arrange the vents, two of which should be at the bottom of the feet and two at the hands. Into these vent-holes fix tubes, bending them and bringing up to the level of the head. Smear the joints with clay so that the wax may not ooze out when the mould is filled with this material (the next stage). When the wax has hardened, remove the mould, and touch up the surface of the figure, for this wax surface is to give the mould for the final bronze. The vents, pour, ingates, etc., are now settled in such positions as will enable the bronze to reach each portion of the mould, and also to allow the air to escape. These vents, pours, etc., are represented at this stage by rolls or rods of wax attached to the figure. The whole is then coated with a composition formed of the burnt core of ox horns (or pounded ox bones), a similar quantity of " gesso of tripoli " (plaster and tripoli clay), a fourth part of iron filings, mixed together with a solution of washed horse or cow dung. The latter is used because it gives particles of hay in a convenient form, which when the mould is burnt become charred and so render the material porous. This composition is painted over the wax with hog-hair brushes in successive coats until a thickness of from $\frac{1}{16}$-inch to $\frac{1}{8}$-inch has been obtained. It is then given a substantial coating of the special clay (mixed with decomposed cloth) and allowed to dry thoroughly, after which the wax is gently melted out and the mould fired. It is then placed in position in a pit, close to the furnace mouth, with the inlet hole (pour) handy to the outlet from the furnace so that the bronze pours easily and is not cooled by too long a journey. Pipes are fitted to the vent-holes and the sand and loam built around the mould, care being taken to bring the vents to the surface and to see they are not choked. Melt the bronze, have all ready, and just before letting out the metal add half a pound more of pewter to every hundred pounds of bronze in the furnace. When cool remove the mould and finish the surface. The method here sketched is practically the same as that described for the " Perseus," but is more concise and gives a few details omitted in that account.

An interesting reference to the casting of his bronze statue of Julius II. occurs in the letters of Michelangelo, showing how uncertain was the process in those days even when undertaken by the most highly skilled men in the profession. " Buonarroto,—Learn that we have cast my statue, and that I was not over fortunate with it, the reason being that Maestro Bernardino (superintendent of artillery to the Florentine Republic) either through ignorance or misfortune failed to melt the metal sufficiently. It would take too long to explain how it happened : enough that my figure has come out up to the waist, the remainder of the metal—half the bronze, that is to say—having caked in the furnace, as it had not melted ; and to get it out the furnace must

9

be taken to pieces.   I am having this done and this week I shall have it built up again.   Next week I shall recast the upper portion and finish filling the mould, and I believe it will turn out tolerably well after so bad a beginning, though only as the result of the greatest labour, worry, and expense.   I was ready to believe that Maestro Bernardino could melt his metal without fire, so great was my confidence in him : but all the same it is not that he is not a skilled master, or that he did not work with a will.   But he who tries may fail.   His failure has been costly to him as well as to me, for he has disgraced himself to such an extent that he dare not raise his eyes in Bologna."

There is a calm philosophy about this letter which tells of a disappointing failure, quite in keeping with the character of Michelangelo ; one wonders what Cellini would have said of Maestro Bernardino had the figure been his ?

CHAPTER XX.

PROPORTIONATE ENLARGEMENT.

For enlarging a sketch model of 2 or 3 feet high to heroic size, the following method of working with a chassis is generally adopted. Similar frames of proportionate size are erected for each work and the measurements transferred from the smaller to the larger, after being proportionately increased (Fig. 49). The smaller model is fixed firmly to a modelling stand, the top of which must be perfectly level and quite rigid. This is placed conveniently near the large turntable or " banker " which is to hold the large model. A square frame of wood somewhat larger each way than the model is now fastened to the stand upon which the sketch is placed, by means of four uprights. Upon this square, above the head of the figure, mark off a number of divisions similar to those upon a foot rule (Fig. 49). See that the square is true in shape and the divisions perfectly accurate. With a triangular file or a sharp knife cut small V-shaped notches in the top edge of the frame to mark the divisions. Into these notches the plumb-line will fit. The next thing is to erect a similar square frame over the stand upon which the larger work is to stand. This frame must be firmly fixed to the wall or ceiling of the studio, as uprights such as those used for the sketch model would impede the work of modelling or carving. It must also be made larger than the other in proportion to the scale of the two figures. If our sketch is 2 feet high and our enlargement is to be 8 feet, the frame will naturally be four times larger than the frame for the sketch. Each of the divisions will also be four times as large, a $\frac{1}{4}$ of an inch will become 1 inch, 1 inch will become 4 inches and so on. V-shaped notches are cut in the top edge of the frame as before. The frames ready, and accurately placed (use a spirit level to get them quite horizontal), we proceed to take our measurements. These are taken as follows : Joining each pair of corners of the frame and crossing in the centre are two strips of wood. At the central crossing on the upper side a screw is fixed, to which are fastened four plumb-lines, one for each side of the frame. These plumb-lines are fitted into the notches on the edges of the frames and should hang down to within an inch or so of the stands. It is now necessary to prepare a strip of wood for each frame, which will reach to just below the top of the stand (being kept in position thereby) and upon which measurements are set out similar to those upon the frame itself. To the upper end of the strip a T-piece is fixed, which rests upon the frame, and keeps the strip in a vertical position (Fig. 49). We have now a framework over each stand (the one upon which the sketch rests and that which is to hold the enlarged figure), four plumb-lines attached to each frame, and a T-square with proportionate divisions for each frame also. There only remains the two pointing sticks by means of which the distances from the vertical strips to the various parts of the figure are measured. These sticks (one for each work) are flat strips or laths of wood brought to a point by shaving off one side, the point being tipped with metal, and a set of measurements marked upon each strip similar to those already marked upon the particular frame with which it is to be used (Fig. 49). The measurements are first taken upon the small model in the following manner. The T-shaped strip is adjusted on the horizontal frame above, and the plumb-line fitted into a certain notch, the pointer is then used to gauge the distance

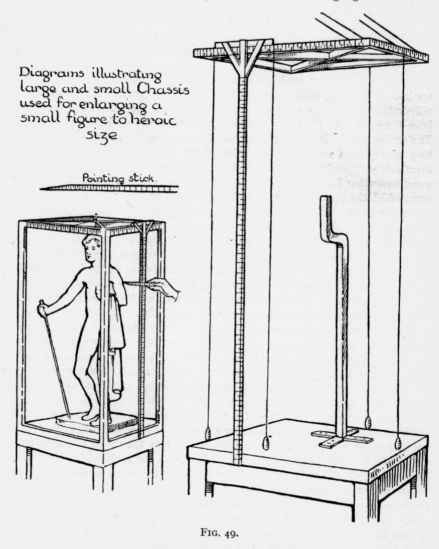

Diagrams illustrating large and small Chassis used for enlarging a small figure to heroic size

Pointing stick.

FIG. 49.

from the plumb-line. The position of the point will be somewhat as follows. Front view, plumb-line in the $4\frac{1}{4}$ notch; " distance down " on the vertical rule, $8\frac{1}{2}$; distance in from plumb-line, measured horizontally with pointing stick, 3. We now turn to the larger frame (which we will presume already contains an armature upon which some clay has been built), and finding a similar point, we build some more clay until it is possible to drive in a peg of wood (similar to those used for modelling the figure) to mark the position of this measurement. This point, having been found from the front, we next turn to the sides and find its position from these points of view—first on the sketch, then on the enlargement. The measurements should be taken systematically in lines as nearly horizontal and vertical as possible, and each measurement marked by a small pencil dot on the sketch model, and by a peg of wood on the enlarged clay model. The pointing stick must be held at right angles to the plumb-line, *i.e.* horizontally. Measurements which are difficult to obtain by means of the chassis may be taken with the callipers, measured on the pointing stick, and so transferred to the larger work by way of the magnified pointing stick and the callipers. When you have sufficient points on your work, the modelling is proceeded with in the ordinary way. The pegs are pressed home and the surface finished as previously described in " Figure Modelling." Needless to say both stands should now revolve freely so that we may study the figures from every viewpoint.

This method is very similar to the one described by Cellini for enlarging a model to the size of a proposed colossal effigy. A framework is set up about the model, and a similar one about the block of marble, after they have been placed side by side on tables of similar size and dimensions. Plumb-lines are used in the same manner as previously described and a succession of points established in precisely the same manner. Vasari speaks of a somewhat simpler arrangement. He mentions a carpenter's square (two straight pieces of wood joined together at right angles), one leg of which laid horizontally upon the table keeps the other vertical, and from this upright the measurements are taken.

Leon Battista Alberti elaborately describes a device invented by him for the purpose of measuring. It consisted of a disc which rested upon the head of the figure projecting to about the level of the shoulders. A series of equal divisions are marked round the circumference, plumb-lines are fastened to the centre, and a long strip of wood projects beyond the disc, revolving on the centre like the hand of a clock. This strip is divided in a similar manner to the circumference of the disc, and another plumb-line slides along it, so that projecting points may be measured. The use of the vertical measuring strip and the pointing stick is understood.

CHAPTER XXI.

A SURVEY OF HISTORIC SCULPTURE.

I. SCULPTURE IN ANCIENT EGYPT AND THE MIDDLE AND FAR EAST.

Pre-historic.—Sculpture, prior to the Egyptian of about 4000 B.C., is practically negligible, except that it shows the development of human thought and ideas.

Dynastic.—The history of Egypt began with the so-called Ancient Empire from about 4000 B.C. to 3000 B.C., followed by the Middle Empire from 3000 to 2000 B.C., and the New Empire from 1700 to 1100 B.C. After these a long period of decadence ensued, arrested from 720 to 525 B.C. (the Saïte Period) by a brilliant but brief renaissance. In 525 B.C. Egypt was conquered by the Persians, since when she has never regained her independence. Many examples of Egyptian sculpture have survived—statues in stone, bronze, and terra-cotta, and bas-reliefs representing religious ceremonies, scenes from daily life, or the soul's journey to the land of the departed.

The work of the Ancient period is more directly inspired by nature than is that of the later periods, probably because the rule of the priesthood had not yet bound the artist's hands with those bonds of convention so apparent in most Egyptian work.

In the Middle period the figures become stiffer, more attenuated and conventional, which tendency is even more accentuated in the New Empire. The brief Saïte Period sees a return to the traditions of the Ancient Empire.

Characteristics.—The dominant notes throughout Egyptian art are size and permanence. Deeply embedded in their minds was a belief in a future life. Eternity meant more to them than time, and so their stone takes on the stamp of the eternal. Gigantic tombs such as the Pyramids, temples with many massive columns, and strong sloping walls, even the figures and bas-reliefs, have a static rigidity, a stiffness and lack of movement, which though not lacking in decorative quality and architectural fitness is yet fraught with this sense of permanence (Plates XXIV. and XXV.).

Cavo-relievo.—The relief work is known as cavo-relievo—an outline is sunk around the figures, and the modelling expressed by a simple rounding of the forms which nowhere stand out from the slab in which they are carved. These reliefs were coloured, and though stiff and archaic yet possess a decorative fitness that harmonises well with their colossal and severe surrounding (Plate XXIV.).

Assyria and Chaldæa.—It cannot be ascertained with any degree of certainty whether the art of Assyria and Chaldæa was influenced by that of

(118)

Egypt. There is a dissimilarity in the two that suggests a separate development. Chaldean, and later, Assyrian figures possess a muscular vigour, almost brutal, that is far removed from the suave attenuated types of the Egyptians. The Chaldean reliefs found at Susa and Tello, and those from Nineveh (some of which are in the British Museum) are very much alike in character and treatment, although the latter are some fifteen centuries later. The Nineveh bas-reliefs commemorate in alabaster the activities and victories of the Assyrian kings. Herein lies one of the differences between Assyrian and Egyptian sculpture. In the latter their deities are the principal actors, whereas in Assyrian the kings occupy these positions, kings engaged in carnage and torture, and glorying in butchery. The gods of Egypt are more, pacific. Assyrian work was mostly in relief, both low and high ; there are but few statues remaining, one of which (a priest) is in the British Museum. The sculptures found at Nimroud (Plate XXVI.), Khorsabad, and Koyunjik date from between 1290 B.C. and some time prior to 538 B.C.—when Nineveh was destroyed. The hunting scene from Nineveh (in the British Museum) depicting horses, men, dogs, and lions, in bas-relief, is a wonderful example of decorative sculpture, the animals in particular being beautifully drawn and modelled, whilst the relief treatment is excellent. There is also a fine decorative quality in the winged bulls with human heads, and the monsters with the heads of eagles, well worthy of careful study. The Assyrians differed from the Egyptians in that they were men of action, " mighty hunters " and warriors, rather than men of peace and contemplation thinking of the future rather than the present, and this difference is stamped upon their art. The treatment of the lions, horses, and winged figures and decorative trees in Plate XXVI. is worthy of careful consideration.

Persian and Phœnician.—Persian art, which lasted for barely two centuries, was distinctly affected by the Chaldean and Assyrian ; the bas-reliefs from the palaces of Susa and Persepolis are evidence of this, though at the same time there is a delicacy and quietness in the subject and the treatment that points to Greek influence. Of a distinctive Phœnician art there is little if any trace ; they were traders who served a useful purpose in carrying works of art from one land to another. Their own work was but a moderate imitation of Egyptian, Assyrian, and Greek.

Indian.—The rock-cut temples of India are interesting, as they afford a record of the rise and progress of religious thought, particularly Buddhism, for a period of 1000 years, or more. The art of a nation is a sure index to the thoughts and aspirations of its people. The earliest of these temples dates from the reign of Asoka, 263 to 229 B.C., and the latest from 12th century A.D. The Buddhistic caves cover the period from the middle of the 3rd century B.C. to the end of the 7th century A.D., the Brahmanical from the 7th century to the 8th century A.D., and the Jain from the 5th or 6th to the 12th century A.D. The work on these temples is highly conventionalised and abstract. Religious restraint was obviously exercised even as with the Egyptians, but there is a fine feeling for line and the ornament is rich and profuse. The figures are somewhat crude and distorted in pose, though often introduced with telling effect.

II. ANCIENT GREEK SCULPTURE.

Greek progress in art was very rapid, but little more than two centuries elapsed between the origin of sculpture in marble and its culmination in the work of Pheidias.   Marble was plentiful in the islands of the Archipelago, and this was undoubtedly a determining factor in the development of the national genius.   The rapid progress is partly explained by the existence of an earlier Mycenæan art, which together with that of Assyria and Egypt, influenced the art of Ionian and Asiatic Greece, which again had its effect upon Greece proper.

After the invasion of Greece by the armies of Darius and Xerxes (490 to 479 B.C.) the national genius gathered fresh impetus.   They set about rebuilding and restoring the work which their enemies had sacked or destroyed.

In the temple of Aphaia at Ægina, 480 to 470 B.C., are some of the earliest examples of Greek statuary at its best.   The western pediment (of which casts are in the British Museum) was filled with splendid work in marble.   The figures are well modelled, showing a knowledge far in advance of previous work, while the poses are vigorous and spirited.   Greater realism was obtained by using bronze for the weapons and by the addition of colour.   The temple of Theseus at Athens was decorated with sculptured representations of his exploits.   Casts are in the British Museum.   The frieze and the metopes are excellent in composition and show a remarkable knowledge of the figure.   It is quite possible that Pheidias was engaged upon this temple as a young man.

The Parthenon is the culmination of a style of art perhaps the most intellectual the world has ever known.   Little emotion can be traced in Greek art. Almost cold in its intellectual beauty, it yet reached a pinnacle of perfection where it stands alone.   Line, form, mass, light, and shadow exquisitely proportioned and balanced, combine to produce a series of masterpieces of reasoned Art.   The frieze from the Parthenon is to be seen complete (as far as it now exists) in the British Museum, some parts in the original marble, the rest in plaster.   There are some 335 feet remaining and nowhere do we find repetition. The metopes, contrasting as they did with the severe lines of the triglyphs, and the entablature are splendid examples of figure grouping for architectural effect. While the frieze is in low relief, the metopes are partly in alto-relievo and partly in the round, the lofty position of the latter making a bolder treatment necessary, which was at once recognised by the æsthetic Greek sculptor.   Contests between Centaurs and Lapithæ, Greeks and Amazons, gods and giants form the subjects, and more harmonious groups cannot be imagined in the spaces they occupy.   In the pediments we find the torsos of Ilissos and Theseus (Plate XXVII.), both of which are wonderful in their realisation of form and graceful movement.   The "Fates" (Plate XXVII.), which adorned the east pediment, are perhaps unrivalled as a rendering of drapery upon the human form.   It is hardly to be conceived that Pheidias carved all these works himself during the sixteen years or so that the Parthenon was building.   Others must have worked under his direction, but who they were we do not know, for his was the master mind from whence emanated those marvellous specimens of the sculptor's art. Ancient writers tell us that the masterpieces of Pheidias were his chryseliphantine (gold and ivory) statues of "Athene," which stood in the Parthenon, and of "Zeus" (seated) in the temple of Olympia.   Both have now disappeared.

Myron and Polyclitus were contemporary with Pheidias, and though both contributed to the plastic expression of Greek genius, they failed to emancipate

PLATE XXVI.

ASSYRIAN RELIEFS FROM THE PALACE OF ASHUR-NASIR-PAL AT CALAH (Nimrûd).

PLATE XXVII.

(a) Figures of the Fates from the East Pediment.

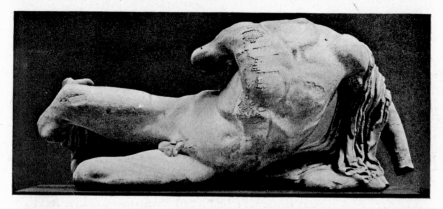

(b) Figure of Illisos from the West Pediment.

(c) Figure of Theseus from the East Pediment.

GREEK SCULPTURE FROM THE PARTHENON.

PLATE XXVIII.

"A MAENAD IN FRENZY." GREEK SCULPTURE IN RELIEF.

PLATE XXIX.

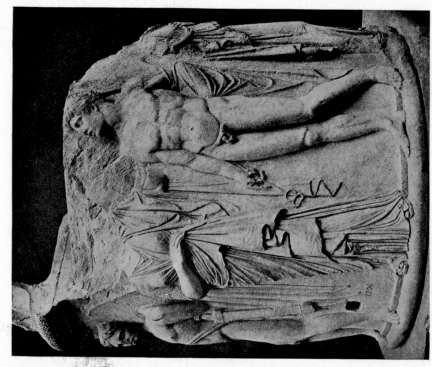

(b) SCULPTURES ON THE DRUM OF A COLUMN.
From the Second Temple of Artemis at Ephesus (Greek).

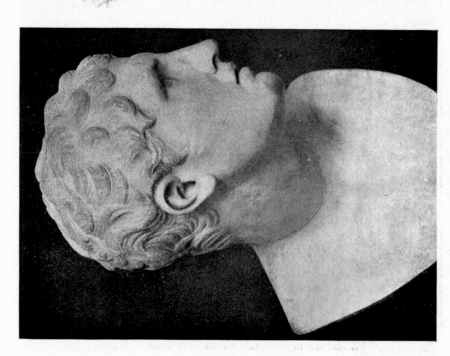

(a) HEAD OF A YOUNG MAN (Greek).

themselves so completely from the archaic influence of earlier work as he did. Myron's " Discobolus " has considerable movement and is strong in its rendering of muscular action.

It is customary with many writers to speak of a decline in Greek art after the time of Pheidias, but it is hardly a decline so much as an inevitable change corresponding with the development of thought and idea. There is a calm dignity, an austere restraint in all the work of Pheidias that, compared with later work, seems almost cold and detached. But the work of Pheidias was as inevitable an expression of the thought of his time, as the work of any other period. With a change of thought in Greece came a change in its sculptural expression.

Art is always the expression of the thoughts and aspirations of the age to which it belongs, and the work of Scopas and Praxiteles evinces the trend of Greek ideas. There is more emotion, and less of the cold, detached, godlike calm in their work than in that of their immediate predecessors. " Hermes carrying the youthful Dionysus," by Praxiteles, is a characteristic example of the graceful, almost feminine beauty that marks this era. The "Heroic Head" (Plate XXIX.), with its deep-set, thoughtful eyes, projecting brows, and some-what sadly parted lips, suggests this period. The " Gladiator " or " Warrior," a cast of which is in most Art schools, is probably a copy of one of the bronzes of Praxiteles, by Agusis of Ephesus. The beautifully draped " Victory " of Samothrace belongs to about 306 B.C. and is obviously of the school of Scopas. There is energy and movement in the body, and a fine contrast between the flutter of the wind-swept drapery, and the simplicity of that which adheres to the forms beneath. It ranks with the " Fates " as a masterpiece of classic drapery. There is no evidence of the " decline " of Greek art here. Another exquisite example of drapery in movement is shown in Plate XXVIII. The sculptured drum from the Temple of Artemis (Diana) at Ephesus (Plate XXIX.) is a further example of a wonderful blend of rounded forms, and the more detailed complex lines of drapery. Emotion is expressed in a number of funeral stelæ which are among the most delicate and restrained of the productions of Attic sculptors of the 4th century.

Alexander the Great succeeded his father Philip in 336 B.C., and as the result of his conquests Athens ceased to be the centre of Greek art. Closer contact with the Oriental nations whom Alexander conquered brought a further change in the thought and outlook of the Greeks which naturally affected their artistic expression. The serene strength of Pheidias, the somewhat melancholy grace of Praxiteles, the passion of Scopas, and the elegance of Lysippus gives place to the expression of deep emotion and a closer rendering of the individuality of the model. In the " Laocoon " emotional expression is carried about as far as it is safe to do so in plastic art. The general characteristics then of Hellen-istic as distinct from the earlier Hellenic sculpture is emotion, carried almost to the stage when it becomes agitation in some works.

Along these lines Greek sculpture developed and the same characteristics are carried over into the Roman work which follows. Besides the marble and bronze work, the terra-cotta figurines produced in Greece from Mycenæn times onward are worthy of notice. The finest are those of Tanagra, dating from the close of the 4th century B.C. They are generally more playful, as though they formed an outlet for the sculptor's lighter fancies, while his deeper ambitions found a medium of expression in marble.

The Greeks were intellectual rather than spiritual. Beauty formed their ideal, and this ideal found a perfect medium of expression in marble. The human form was regarded with a love and a reverence unapproached by earlier peoples. Their sculptors were more concerned with perfection of form and proportion than with mystic attributes wherewith to suggest the spiritual and the eternal. The work of Pheidias is the apogee of Hellenic thought pure and simple. That of Praxiteles, Scopas, and Lysippus marks the introduction of philosophy and subtlety of thought ; outside influences have made the Greek more introspective, and his outlook becomes less joyful as he becomes more meditative. The final stage in Attic sculpture, before it merges into Græco-Roman, tends towards dissatisfaction. It seems to indicate a yearning after ideals higher and nobler than mere physical beauty. The spiritual element has become more insistent and demands expression. During the Roman period we see various phases, first a return to the colder classic, then a revival of the emotional and passionate, followed by a further renaissance of the Hellenic, until finally we come to the ascetic symbolism of Early Christian art, where the material gives place entirely to the spiritual.

III. ANCIENT ROMAN SCULPTURE.

Somewhere about 1000 B.C. a party of emigrants from Lydia in Asia Minor settled in central Italy, and, intermingling with the natives, founded the Etruscan federation. A flourishing civilisation was developed, of which ample evidence remains in the form of ruined temples, tombs ornamented with reliefs, statues, sarcophagi, bronzes, and gold ornaments. The vases known as Etruscan were largely imported from Attica. The work of the Etrurians, while betraying its Greek origin, has yet a distinct character lent by the Italian element. More vigorous and realistic than Grecian work, it aims at the individual rather than the ideal and typical. Conquered by the Romans in 283 B.C. their artists worked for the victors, and helped in the formation of the Roman style. Later the services of the subject Greeks were enlisted and a more distinct Hellenic influence was introduced. The sculpture consists largely of copies of existing statues, and for this we are grateful to them, for otherwise many of the works mentioned by Pliny, Pausanius, and other writers, would never have been known except from their writings. The development of Roman art is rather a continuation of the native Italian than a mere degenerate copy of the Greek. It has been said that the Romans cared little for art except in so far as it pandered to their love of ostentation and display. Even if this is the case they certainly encouraged their artists who displayed considerable activity if one may judge from the works remaining. Various influences may be traced by a careful examination of Roman sculpture. The head of the youthful Augustus is as simple and as restrained as the typical work of Greece. From the reign of Claudius a more vigorous, animated style comes into being, examples of which are the bas-reliefs on the Arch of Titus, and the Trajan Column (A.D. 114) which further bears an inscription in Roman lettering providing us with our standard type to-day. Realistic flower, leaf, and fruit forms were also introduced, breaking away from the more conventional acanthus, honeysuckle, and palm renderings of the Greeks. This tendency was short-lived, for after the death of Trajan in 117 A.D. an archaistic reaction set in, manifesting itself under Hadrian by the production of a number of copies of classic statues and ornament. The

PLATE XXX.

STATUE OF JULIUS CAESAR (Roman) IN THE NAPLES MUSEUM.

PLATE XXXI.

SCULPTURED TOMB IN THE CHURCH OF SANT' APOLLINARE IN CLASSE,
RAVENNA (Byzantine).

ROMANESQUE CARVING.

PLATE XXXII.

CASTS OF GOTHIC ROUNDELS AND CARVED PANELS FROM NOTRE DAME, PARIS.

Plate XXXIII.

Detail of Carved Wooden Screen, High Ham Church, Somerset.

middle of the second century brings a further degeneration of Roman sculpture which falls under the influence of a sort of orientalised Greek art, which though as yet but little known was probably to some extent the source of Byzantine work.   It will be seen from the foregoing brief sketch, how erroneous it is to classify Roman art as a sort of degenerate Greek.   It has characteristics of its own, even though it bears unmistakable evidences of Greek influence.   They did things which would never have been permitted by the finer taste of the Grecians, as representing nobles and their wives as deities, and carving the men nude as though heroic.   This is somewhat parallel to the English sculptors who gave us statesmen and other dignitaries garbed as Roman warriors.   But despite its shortcomings the contribution of the Romans to art is not without its significance, particularly in architecture.   Plate XXX. is a characteristic example of Roman sculpture.

IV. EARLY CHRISTIAN AND BYZANTINE SCULPTURE.

The early Christians were opposed to sculpture in the round, because idols were worshipped in heathen temples.   The church of Santa Sophia at Constantinople is decorated with beautiful mosaics, and generally colour rather than form is the keynote.   The Iconoclasts destroyed a number of works of art, and striking terror into the Byzantine artists caused them to flee from the Empire. The suppression of the Iconoclasts about 850 A.D. brought about an artistic renaissance which lasted through the 10th and part of the 11th centuries. Sculpture was, however, not encouraged, but mosaics, enamels, bas-reliefs in ivory and metal, and goldsmiths' work, exist which show great technical skill and considerable beauty.   Severe restrictions were set upon the artist by the religious authorities, and art became stereotyped, as might be expected.   An ascetic severity almost archaic marks the work of the period, arising out of the importance attached to the spiritual element in religion.   Art was looked upon merely as a medium for lifting the thoughts above mundane things.   Too much beauty would (they felt) tend to hold the mind in contemplation of itself, instead of leading it past the representation into the realm of spiritual ideas.   Art was a language, a symbolic language, wherewith to teach, to suggest the mysteries of religion, to which it was subordinate, and in no way to be compared.   Art was not to be practised for its own sake, it was the handmaid of religion.   Physical beauty was regarded as a snare and a delusion ; only in so far as it could be used to embody religious teaching was it to be admitted.   We have here a parallel to the Art of the Egyptians, and of other essentially religious peoples.   Plate XXXI. (a) illustrates the symbolism that plays so important a part in Early Christian decoration.

V. ROMANESQUE AND GOTHIC SCULPTURE.

The essential difference between Romanesque and Gothic architecture is, that the former is solid looking, with round arches and large surfaces of stone, while the latter is light and graceful with a tendency to soar upwards, and many pointed windows.   Romanesque is horizontal and static, Gothic is vertical and dynamic in suggestion.   This architectural difference has its effect upon the sculpture of the two styles.   The priesthood exercised a dominating influence during both periods, but it was less rigid during the Gothic.   The decoration of Romanesque churches was largely the work of the monks.   In the Gothic, lay sculptors were employed, who were not so closely bound by the ecclesiastical authorities, and were, therefore, allowed more scope for imaginative work. There is considerable dignity and decorative quality in Romanesque sculpture, which seems inspired rather by other work than by the study of nature. The most powerful influence was Roman, but there are also unmistakable signs of Byzantine, Arabian, Persian, and further of the interlacings and complicated ornament peculiar to the art of northern countries. The result is consequently conventional and abstract. The figures are usually stiff and elongated, the drapery thin and archaic, and the ornament a mixture of motifs culled from other styles. The transition from Romanesque and Gothic shows a gradual return to natural forms, and the change is distinctly marked when Gothic art reaches maturity. Plate XXXII. illustrates the transition, while Fig. 50 and Plate XXXIII. show the further development of Gothic. There is no space here to trace the growth of the style in the various European countries or to indicate the slight but characteristic modifications peculiar to racial and other differences. The illustrations are merely sufficient to show the broad tendencies of the Gothic style.

VI. ITALIAN RENAISSANCE SCULPTURE.

The art of the Renaissance was inspired by a vigorous revival of the Classic spirit blended with the Gothic traditions which had been the stimulus of the earlier artists. This blend is evinced in the pulpit of the Baptistery of Pisa by *Niccola Pisano* (born between 1205 and 1207, died 1278), the general form of which is Gothic, while the decoration, particularly the bas-reliefs, is decidedly antique in treatment. He seems to have been the first Italian sculptor to depart from the Gothic tradition. *Andrea Pisano* (1270-1345) carried on this tradition from which neither his son Nino, nor his pupil Balduccio di Pisa make any attempt to break away.

The Siennese school may be distinctly traced to Niccola Pisano, who went to Sienna to carve a pulpit and so brought his influence to bear upon the local guild of stone workers. The façade of Orvieto Cathedral is the work of the Siennese school and bears the unmistakable stamp of Niccola and Giovanni Pisano, though the later work shows a steady improvement.

Tino da Camaino and *Niccolo d'Arrezzo* are two well-known Siennese sculptors of this time.

After the decline of the Pisan school there is a lapse of half a century or so, before the rise of the Florentine, of which *Ghiberti* (1378-1465) was the foremost amongst the early men. His bronze gates for the Baptistery are well known. He was also responsible for a number of other works including monuments, statues, tombs, etc., but his best-known productions are undoubtedly his gates. Plate XXXV. is an example of his relief work in bronze.

Jacopo della Quercia (1371-1438) was an unsuccessful competitor for the gates of the Baptistery. His reputation was established by the Fonte Gaia at Sienna, his fellow-citizens being so impressed that they named him Jacopo della Fonte (Jacopo of the Fountain). Vecchietta, 1412-1480, painter, sculptor, architect and goldsmith, was a pupil of della Quercia. In the Duomo of Sienna is a bronze tabernacle, and in the Florentine gallery of bronzes an effigy of Mariano Sozzino, both somewhat hard in style. Plate XXXIV. is typical of his school.

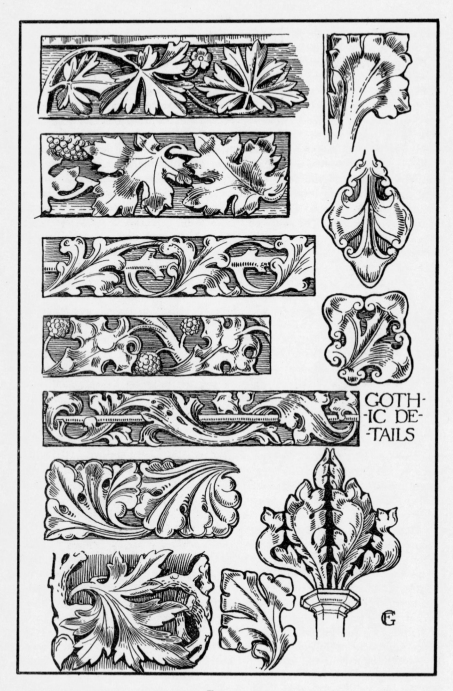

GOTH-
-IC DE-
-TAILS

Fig. 50.

Donatello (1386-1466) received his first instruction in the shop of a gold-smith, as did many of the artists of that day. Later he worked in the studio of Ghiberti for a short time, but his work betrays little if any of the characteristics of that master, for, though realistic, his productions are marked by an earnest severity more in keeping with the true character of sculpture than are those of Ghiberti. The forms beneath the drapery are manifest in the figures of St. John and St. Mark, and more plainly still in the splendid " St. George " in Or San Michele. Three statues executed for Santa Maria del Fiore, the "St. John," the "David," called "Zuccone," and the "Prophet Jeremiah" are eminently statuesque and suitable for the architectural positions they occupy. Following these come two more statues of St. John the Baptist, almost nude studies from the living model. The Bargello Baptist in particular is an emaciated figure, thin and fragile. This power of characterisation which distinguishes Donatello from all his predecessors finds its most complete expression in his portrait busts. The so-called " Niccolo da Uzzano " is a masterpiece of character rendering. A bust of " St. John " (Berlin) and a female head in terra-cotta (S.K.M.) are other fine examples of his sympathetic treatment. Many other works came from his hand, including the famous equestrian statue of " Gattamelata," but his bas-reliefs display his wonderful skill perhaps more completely than his works in the round. He excelled particularly in a very flat relief known as " stiacciato " where the effect depends upon exquisite drawing combined with delicate modelling and a subtle management of planes (Plate XXXVIII.). " St. Cecilia," the " Infant St. John," and eight circular shields executed for Cosimo de Medici are good examples of his ability in this direction. Many specimens of his work are still in existence, for during his eighty years of life he laboured continuously, and exercised a decided influence over the work of his contemporaries and successors. Amongst the pupils of this great sculptor were *Manni d'Antonio di Banco, Bertoldo di Giovanni, Vellano da Padua, Michelozzo Michelozzi, Verrocchio,* and *Desiderio da Settignano.*

Desiderio da Settignano (1425-1464) was, as previously stated, a pupil of Donatello. His work was highly finished, delicate, and graceful. His monument to Carlo Marzuppini in Santa Croce is richly ornamented without being ostentatious. The bust of Marietta Pulla Strozzi is also highly finished with well-realised forms and rich drapery. Some of his relief work challenges comparison with that of his master (Plate XXXIV.).

Mino da Fiesole (1430-1484) worked with Settignano and in a measure adopted or developed a similar style. As delicate and highly finished as Desiderio's work, he has yet an individual quality which distinguishes it from that of his contemporaries. There is a beautiful altar of his in the Cathedral at Fiesole, a fine tabernacle in the church of Santa Maria in Trastevere at Rome, and a similar one in the Duomo of Volterra.

Verrocchio (1435-1485), the master of Leonardo da Vinci Lorenzo di Credi and Perugino, and himself the pupil of Donatello, is best known by his fine equestrian statue of Colleone at Venice. Other works of his are a bronze statue of David in the National Museum, Florence, a terra-cotta crucifix at South Kensington, and a bronze boy with a dolphin on the fountain in the Cortile of the Palazzo Vecchio, Florence. He is reputed to have been the first Renaissance sculptor to use plaster of Paris for the manufacture of moulds, another revival of ancient methods, as burnt gypsum had been used prior to the Renaissance.

PLATE XXXIV.

(b) MADONNA AND CHILD IN RELIEF. Ascribed to Desiderio da Settignano (15th Century).

(a) CARVED COPPER FRONT REPRESENTING THE LABOURS OF ADAM AND EVE. School of Jacopo della Quercia (15th Century).

PLATE XXXV.

(a) ENAMELLED TERRA-COTTA RELIEF OF THE ADORATION OF THE MAGI.
By Luca della Robbia (15th Century).

(b) DETAIL OF RELIEFS ON DOORWAY TO THE BAPTISTERY, FLORENCE CATHEDRAL.
By Lorenzo Ghiberti (15th Century).

Plate XXXVI.

Terra-cotta Relief of the Birth of Saint John the Baptist. Attributed to Benedetto da Majano (15th Century).

PLATE XXXVII.

(b) MARBLE "CUPID." By Michelangelo (Early 16th Century).

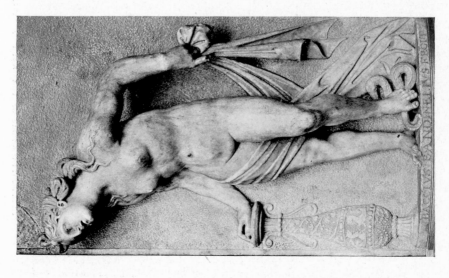

(a) MARBLE FIGURE OF VENUS. By Baccio
Bandinelli (16th Century).

The work of the Della Robbia family is justly famed. *Luca della Robbia* (1400-1482) was, like so many of the artists of his time, first apprenticed to a goldsmith. The bas-reliefs for the organ gallery in the Duomo at Florence are wonderfully free in action ; the figures graceful in pose, and the drapery flowing in harmonious lines, seem fraught with the spirit of music. There are casts of this in South Kensington Museum. After executing a few more works in marble Luca turned his attention to terra-cotta which he coloured and glazed (Plate XXXV.), thereby rendering his work more permanent even than marble. He was joined by his nephew *Andrea* (1435-1525), whose five sons continued to produce the glazed terra-cotta that Luca had invented. It is therefore exceedingly difficult to assign the numerous examples which exist to their particular authors. Many are, however, attributed to Luca and to Andrea, whilst many more are simply known as della Robbia ware. Luca is responsible for the relief of the " Resurrection " above the northern gates of the Tribune of the Duomo, and the " Ascension " over the southern gates. A charming relief of the " Madonna adoring the infant Christ," in the convent of San Marco, Florence ; a Madonna, a " St. Dominic," and a " St. Peter the Martyr," in the arch of the great door of San Domenico of Urbino are also his, together with many others. To Andrea is attributed a circular relief of the Madonna and Child in the large portal of the cathedral of Pistoja, whilst to the family generally belong a large number of works scattered over Italy, besides those which have found their way into other countries. At South Kensington there are some fifty examples of della Robbia ware, well worthy of study for the beauty of the modelling and their charm of colour.

Antonia Rossellini (1427-1479) was the only one of five brothers to achieve fame as a sculptor. Though reported to have been a pupil of Donatello, he developed a style distinctly his own. There is a charming tomb in San Miniato of " Jacopo di Portogallo," and another almost identical, except for the addition of an exquisite relief of the " Resurrection," in the church of Santa Maria di Monte, Naples. Other excellent works of Rossellini's are the bas-relief of the " Nativity " in the church of Santa Maria, Naples, a circular relief of the " Madonna adoring the Infant Saviour," in the Florentine gallery, and the monument to Bishop Lorenzo Roverella, in the church of San Giogio at Ferrara.

Benedetto da Maiano or *Majano* (1442-1498) is the only one of three brothers worthy of mention. One of his best works is the sarcophagus of Filippo Strozzi in Santa Maria Novello, the reliefs and the supporting angels being beautifully carved. The altar of San Bartolo in the church of Sant' Agostino is another rich example of his work. Plate XXXVI. is attributed to him.

Andrea Sansovino (1460-1529), the son of a labourer, was himself employed as a cattle herd in his childhood. Too intelligent and thoughtful, however, for this occupation, he busied himself by drawing in the sand and modelling in clay the animals he was set to watch. A Florentine citizen, seeing him thus engaged, was struck by the boy's bent for art and arranged for him to study in the Art School of the Medici garden. Sansovino was one of those artists in whose work architecture and sculpture are harmoniously blended. The Chapel of the Sacrament in Santa Spirito designed by him is richly adorned with his statues, reliefs, etc., the whole scheme culminating in a " Pieta " in mezzo-relievo over the altar.

Michelangelo Buonarroti (1475-1564) is the giant who overtops the sculptors of the Renaissance. Sculptor, painter, architect, engineer, and poet, his work in either sphere was excellent enough to establish a reputation. He was, however, first and foremost a sculptor, form being undoubtedly his mode of expression ; colour had nothing like the same appeal for him. In his paintings he relies upon form rather than colour, which is always somewhat harsh and unpleasing. He was articled in his youth to Domenico Ghirlandajo, but before his time had expired the contract was broken by mutual consent, for the pupil had out-sped his master. At the age of fifteen he went to live at the Medici Palace, where he studied the antique sculpture placed by Lorenzo Medici in the garden of his palace for the benefit of artists. Amongst his earliest efforts was a Cupid (Plate XXXVII.).

In Rome he carved the " Pietà," a wonderful conception in which the nude figure of Jesus lying across the knees of the Madonna forms a striking contrast to the voluminous drapery that envelopes her. David is a beautifully constructed figure of colossal size, a masterpiece of anatomical analysis, worthy of careful study for the superb manner in which essentials have been realised. The tombs of Guiliano and Lorenzo di Medici are extraordinary personifications of sombre, contemplative power, dominating a group of strong, almost violently posed figures, symbolising " Day " and " Night," " Evening " and " Dawn." The figure of Moses prepared for the tomb of Julius II. is another tremendous conception, full of " repressed movement " and vibrating with wrath and passion. The two Slaves designed for the same tomb are also full of movement, and though unfinished are splendid examples of the sculptor's art. There is no space here to deal with all the work produced by this restless genius during his eighty odd years of strenuous activity.

Baccio Bandinelli (1488-1559) was a man of a jealous temperament. One of the many students who studied from Michelangelo's cartoon, " Soldiers Surprised while Bathing," Vasari tells us that Baccio, having obtained all the benefit he could from it, tore the cartoon so that his companions should not benefit equally. His chief works are " Hercules and Cocus," a marble copy of the " Laocoon," " Orpheus in Inferno," " St. Peter," and " David killing Goliath." But in none of his works does he reach a very high level. Benvenuto Cellini in his " Autobiography " mentions him frequently, for of all his enemies Baccio Bandinelli was the one he hated most fervently. Plate XXXVII. is an example of his work.

Benvenuto Cellini (1500-1572), goldsmith, metal-worker, sculptor, and bronzefounder, was a truculent, swaggering fellow. The bulk of his work was in the precious metals, but some of his sculpture is worthy of mention. " Perseus," perhaps the best, is a bronze figure, and the accounts he gives in his " Autobiography " and in his treatises of the difficulties he overcame when casting it are extremely interesting. A " Crucifix " in marble is well modelled, a bronze bust of Duke Cosimo is also good, while a bronze portrait of Bindo Altoviti wno the praise of Michelangelo. His works in metal are technically unrivalled : the salt-cellar in repoussé gold, made for King Francis, is really marvellous. The chalice made for the Pope is also very fine. He was further commissioned to make the Papal coins, and the designs he produced certainly justified the Pope's selection.

Giovanni da Bologna (1524-—) was a native of France who settled in Italy and took high rank among his contemporaries. While most of these were engaged in slavish imitations of the great Florentine sculptor, Giovanni retained

PLATE XXXVIII.

(a) TERRA-COTTA RELIEF OF THE VIRGIN AND CHILD. By Donatello (15th Century).

(b) FIGURE RELIEF ON A TOMB. School of Donatello (15th Century).

PLATE XXXIX.

(*a*) THE TOMB OF PHILIPPE POT, NOW IN THE LOUVRE (French, 15th Century).

(*b*) THE TOMB OF FRANCIS II. IN NANTES CATHEDRAL. By Michel Colombe (15th Century).

a classic simplicity and a beauty of form due to his deep study of the antique. The " Rape of the Sabines," the " Hercules and the Centaur " both contain some excellent modelling. " Mercury," a bronze figure in the National Museum at Florence, is exquisite in its movement, while the forms are classic and restrained in feeling. South Kensington Museum contains a reproduction of this figure. " Samson and the Philistines," " Bacchus," and " Victory " are further examples of the work of this sculptor, who was the last outstanding figure of the Italian Renaissance. After its culmination in Michelangelo there is a steady decline, for no one appeared who was great enough to maintain the lofty standard set by this titanic genius. Giovanni da Bologna stemmed for awhile the receding tide, but after him there were no sculptors strong enough to affect the retrograde movement, and the glorious epoch known as the Italian Renaissance came to an end.

VII. FRENCH SCULPTURE.

The early sculpture of France displays the same characteristics that mark the sculpture of other European countries. Large religious compositions over the tympana of porches, and " histories " and figures of men and animals carved on the friezes and capitals of columns occur in the Romanesque style. The transition from Romanesque to Gothic is gradual, and many works contain the characteristic features of both styles. But the contrast between the fully developed Gothic and the typical Romanesque is very striking. The sculptors who adorned the cathedrals of Rheims, Amiens, Chartres, and Paris were students of nature. The figures, draperies, flowers, and foliage wherewith they decorated their buildings are studied from the natural forms and are in marked contrast to the conventional forms used by the Romanesque carvers. France is particularly rich in Gothic remains. The aim of the sculptor was to teach. Scenes from the Scriptures and legends of the saints ; representations of the seasons, of animal and vegetable forms, of the arts, crafts, and sciences and allegorical renderings of the virtues and vices may be found amongst his works.

At the beginning of the fourteenth century French art underwent a change. A more secular feeling took the place of religious zeal, and realism became the dominant factor. There is a period of inactivity corresponding to the Hundred Years War after this, when little was done. Then we come to the so-called " Well of Moses," a six-sided structure which formed the base of a " Calvary." Each side bears a life-size figure of the six great prophets who predicted the coming of Christ : Moses, David, Jeremiah, Zechariah, Daniel, and Isaiah. This is the work of *Claus Sluter*, a Dutchman, who was responsible for a number of other good figures, in which the drapery is voluminous and well studied. He was assisted by *Claus de Werve*. The effigy of Philippe Pot, lying fully armed on a slab of marble borne on the shoulders of eight " Pleurants " (Plate XXXIX.) is a remarkable work also attributed to these two sculptors. In the carvings of Sluter and Werve, and also of Jean Ravi and Jean Bouteiller, may be observed a foreshadowing of the coming Renaissance. *Michel Colombe* (1431-1512) raised the standard of French sculpture to a still higher level with a spirit that is still essentially French rather than Italian. His " St. George and the Dragon " in the Louvre is somewhat stiff and rigid, but the " Madonna of Olivet " attributed to him is a work of considerable beauty. This work has all the dignity and restraint of the best of the Gothic, blended with the realism of a later epoch (Plate XXXIX.).

Jean Goujon (about 1510-1572) was the first to introduce the new era of sculpture into France. His figures are slender and graceful and his work generally highly decorative in feeling. "The Fountain of the Innocents" has some reliefs of great delicacy. These reliefs, the "Diana and Stag," and the Caryatides of the Louvre are perhaps his most famous works, and well display his elegant, dainty style. He had a finely developed sense of architectural fitness, and his decorative work combines beautifully with the surrounding structure.

Germain Pilon (1535-1590) possessed most of the grace of Goujon, though he differed considerably in his treatment of drapery, which falls in more voluminous folds, and is studied from heavier material. His "Three Graces," supporting the urn wherein the heart of Henry II. was to rest, is a graceful solution of a difficult problem. The three figures are placed back to back in a triangular arrangement carrying the urn on their heads; they are light and elegant in pose, well varied and tastefully draped.

Other names that occur about this period are *Ligier Richier* (1500-1567), *Jean Waring* (1604-1672), *Simon Guillain* (1581-1658), *Jacques Sarrozin* (1588-1660), who is responsible for the pompous tomb of Henri de Condé; the brothers *François* (1604-1669) and *Michel Anguier* (1612-1686); and *Gilles Guérin* (1606-1678).

Pierre Puget (1622-1694) based his style on Bernini and the Italian successors of Michelangelo. The "Milo of Crotona" is a much debated work, which displays the agony of the athlete who endeavours to release his left hand from the tree which grips it, while trying with his right to push off the lion that has seized his thigh. The relief of "Alexander and Diogenes" is a characteristic example of his vigorous, almost violent art.

François Girardon (1628-1715) executed an equestrian statue of Louis XIV., a tomb of Richelieu, and a leaden bas-relief in the Bassin du Nord at Versailles, all of which are marked by grace and refinement.

Antoine Coysevox (1640-1720) modelled with considerable daring and assurance, especially in his portrait busts, those of "Condé" and "Le Brun" being strong in character. Amongst the tombs executed by him are those to Cardinal Mazarin, to Condé, to Colbert, and to Charles Le Brun. His marbles were finely finished with a flesh-like texture. The brothers *Nicholas* (1658-1733) and *Guillaume* (1678-1746) *Couston* were pupils of Coysevox and both became well-known sculptors. The elder one carved a colossal group of the "Junction of the Seine and the Marne," and a bronze statue of the "Saone." The younger brother was responsible for a bronze statue of the "Rhone," for statues of Louis XIV. and of Cardinal Dubois, and also for the "Horses of Marly" at the entrance to the Champs Elysées.

Edmé Bouchardon (1698-1762) had a fervent reverence for the ancients. His greatest work was perhaps the bronze equestrian statue of Louis XV. which has, however, since been melted to provide metal for cannon. The bas-reliefs from a fountain, of which Plate XL. is one illustration, are charming in modelling and delicate in treatment.

Pigalle (1714-1785) carved the tombs of the Duc d'Harcourt and the Maréchal de Saxe, both of which are grandiloquent, though well composed and skilful in technique. Less ambitious but far more satisfactory is the statue of "Mercury."

Maurice Etienne Falconet (1716-1781) executed a colossal equestrian statue of "Peter the Great" which is still at Leningrad, and this together with his

Plate XL.

Sculptured Reliefs on the Fontaine du Grenelle, Paris. By Bouchardon (18th Century).

PLATE XLI.

(a) Fountain in the Luxembourg Gardens, Paris. By Carpeaux.

(b) "Milon de Crotone." By Pierre Puget.

(c) "Genius Guarding the Secret of the Tomb," By Saint-Marceaux.

French Sculpture of the Nineteenth Century.

" Nymph Descending to the Bath " are his best-known productions. His works provided many models for Sèvres china.

Augustin Pajou (1730-1809) modelled soft and graceful nude figures of which " Psyche " in the Louvre is a good specimen. He also worked considerably in terra-cotta.

Clodion or *Claude Michel* (1738-1814) also modelled in terra-cotta in which medium he produced a number of playful bas-reliefs of satyrs, nymphs, and cupids. He executed a large quantity of work, and was exceedingly popular in his day.

Jean-Antoine Houdon (1744-1828) is best known by his portrait busts, though he is also responsible for some fine statues as " St. Bruno," " Diana," and the seated Voltaire of the Theâtre Français prove. He is said to have produced over two hundred busts, and many of them are well known. They are strong in characterisation and vigorous in modelling.

François Rude (1784-1856) is the next sculptor of outstanding merit. He executed many works of great beauty and originality, of which the best are probably the group on the Arc de l'Etoile, " Maréchal Ney," " Joan of Arc," and the " Neapolitan Fisher Boy." The group " Le Départ " from the Arc de l'Etoile is of colossal size and inspired by patriotic fervour. Some of the figures are beautifully modelled, and altogether the composition is a remarkable piece of sculpture. It is certainly a departure from the suave classical productions of his immediate predecessors.

Antoine Louis Barye (1796-1857) is justly celebrated for his naturalistic rendering of animals. His " Lion and Serpent " in the garden of the Tuileries is an excellent work, while a " Tiger Devouring a Crocodile," " Centaur and the Lapithæ," and many of his smaller bronzes of animals are studiously rendered, and sculpturesque in character.

Emanuel Frémiet (1824-1900) was a pupil of his uncle Rude. At first he confined his attention to animals, the result of which is seen in the beautiful modelling of the horses in his later equestrian statues. Bold in conception and strong in modelling his numerous productions are well worthy of study. " Louis d'Orléans," " Joan of Arc," " St. George and the Dragon," " Meissonier," " Velasquez," " Duguesclin," " St. Michael " on the spire of the church at Mont St. Michel, and the monument to " Raffet " in front of the Louvre, are all fine examples of Frémiet's distinctive style.

Jean Baptiste Carpeaux (1827-1875) was also a pupil in Rude's studio. His sculpture is marked by a consummate knowledge of the human figure. There is a suppleness and a sureness of anatomical construction combined with a beauty of contour that places his work very high in the scale of contemporary sculpture. It may be that occasionally his desire to display his command over the human figure overstepped the limits of good taste. " Ugolino," for instance, a group inspired by Dante's " Inferno," whilst beautiful in anatomical construction and in the poses of the figures, is yet heavy and perhaps a trifle repulsive in its tragic intensity. " The Dance " and " Flora " exhibit, on the other hand, a joyous vitality. Other works are : the " Fountain of the Observatory " (Plate XLI.), a group of four figures representing the four parts of the earth, a statue of " Watteau," and some splendid busts of " Alexandre Dumas," of " Napoleon III.," of " Garnier," of " La Princesse Mathilde," and of the " Marquise de la Valette."

Jules Dalou (1838-1902) is known to fame as the sculptor of the " Triumph of the Republic " in Paris.   It is an unusual group, ornate and elaborate, but impressive, if only for its size.   Superior in every way is the bas-relief of " 1883 at the Chamber of Deputies."   This difficult scene is rendered with consummate skill by a wonderful management of the planes and the perspective.

Charles René De Saint-Marceaux (1845-—) is well known as the sculptor of " Genius Guarding the Secret of the Tomb " (Plate XLI.), a splendidly conceived and strongly modelled figure, well poised on a nicely proportioned pedestal and clasping an urn.   Though full of movement, the figure still suggests a vigilant guardianship, unrelaxing and permanent.   " Daudet " is also well known, as are his monuments to " President Faure " and to " Dumas Fils " and his statue of " Bailly."

Paul Albert Bartholomé (1848-—) achieved fame with his " Monument to the Dead."   It is a dramatic conception, almost brutal in its realisation of the horror of death.   The strong severity of the Egyptian architecture with its rigid inflexible lines only serves to accentuate the hopelessness of the mourning figures.

It is impossible in this short sketch to mention all the sculptors of France up to modern times.   They are numerous and varied in attainments—as *Théophile Barrau*, successful with the nude ; *Alfred Boucher*, whose bronze group " To the Goal " is a skilful rendering of figures in violent action ; *Gustave Michel*, distinguished for his portrait busts and his decorations of the Pont de Passy ; *Charles Verlet*, known for his monument to " Guy de Maupassant " ; *Georges Gordet*, second only to Barye in his rendering of animals—are but a few of the better known of the later men in France.   But no sketch, however brief, would be complete without some mention of *Auguste Rodin*, who by sheer originality of thought and execution has achieved a fame far in advance of all modern sculptors.   It is difficult to place one's contemporaries, and it is for future generations to decide upon the niche in the temple of Fame which Rodin will occupy, but any sculptor capable of modelling " The Burghers of Calais," " St. John the Baptist," " The Iron Age," or " The Thinker " must assuredly occupy a very lofty position amongst the artists of the world, whether ancient or modern.   Plate XLV. is a fine example of his vigorous yet subtle sculpture.

VIII. ENGLISH SCULPTURE.

But little is known of the men who adorned our cathedrals and churches with that wonderful carving which is so characteristic a feature of Gothic Art, and also to a certain extent of the earlier Norman.   We can only judge by the craftsmanship, and cannot fail to be impressed with the keen sense of design, and the fine feeling for treatment of stone and wood.   The ornament is almost invariably in perfect harmony with the surroundings, and obviously the outcome of a correct use of tools and material (Plate XXXIII.).   Peter the Roman is one name that flashes out for a moment associated with the Shrine of Edward the Confessor.   He came to England in 1279, and is supposed to have been engaged on other works besides the shrine, but again the mist deepens, and nothing definite is known.   John Sutton, Thomas Porchalion, John Essex, John Bourde of Corfe Castle, Richard of Reading, Master Cannings of St. Mary Redcliffe, Bristol, are other names appearing in ancient records, but of their work we know nothing.

The first of whom we have any tangible account is Pietro Torregiano, who was responsible for the tomb of Henry VII., completed in 1518 (Plate XLII.). The tomb of Margaret, Countess of Richmond, also in the Abbey ; and the tomb of Dr. Young, Master of the Rolls, in the Rolls Chapel, Chancery Lane, are further specimens of Pietro's work. The latter tomb is in terra-cotta, in which material there are also some fine medallions by this artist at Hampton Court. After Torregiano there follows a further period of obscurity from which a few names faintly emerge as Benedetto da Rovezzano who was engaged upon a tomb for Wolsey. It is doubtful whether he finished it, for nothing remains. Another competitor for this work was Baccio Bandinelli, but his designs were not accepted. Other names that appear are Tyrrel and Richard Stevens. A poor list, indeed, to account for all the work executed prior to 1600, and curiously enough, the only ones to whom we can definitely attribute any particular speci-men are those who had established a reputation in Italy, before coming to England. With the 17th century the record grows clearer. *Nicholas Stone* (1586-1647) is the first English sculptor of importance of whom we know any-thing. The tombs of Bodley at Oxford, Sutton at Charterhouse, Lady Bennet in York Minster, Sir Thomas Drury in Hawstead Church, and many others, came from his chisel. The monuments to Edmund Spenser, to Francis Holles, to Sir George Holles, to Sir George Villiers and his wife, to Isaac Casaubon, and to Dudley Carleton and his wife, in the Abbey, are his also. He was employed on the Banqueting Hall at Whitehall, designed by Inigo Jones, and much other work for the King, who made him master-mason.

Hubert le Sueur, whose bronze statue of Charles I. faces Whitehall, was a Parisian who came to London somewhere about 1628. A pupil of John of Bologna, he is reputed to have been a sculptor of considerable merit, and the workmanship displayed in the statue of Charles I. certainly argues unusual skill ; but except for a bust of Sir Thomas Richardson, and another of Lady Cottingdon, both in Westminster Abbey, nothing else exists whereby to judge him. He seems to have worked mainly in bronze.

Francis Fanelli, a Florentine, has left a few examples of his work, notably the full-length effigies of Abraham Blackleech in Gloucester Cathedral, and of Mrs. Delves at Horsham, the latter being particularly good.

Edward Pierce was an architect as well as a sculptor, and acted as assistant to Wren. His most important works in sculpture were a bust of Oliver Crom-well (a terra-cotta replica of which is in the National Portrait Gallery) and a monument to Sir William Maynard in Little Easton Church, Essex. This monument is typical of the pseudo-classical work of the period.

Caius Gabriel Cibber, the father of Colley Cibber, came to England first to assist the Stones. About the year 1667, however, he started on his own account and was soon busily occupied in carving classical deities and figures from Greek mythology for the adornment of gardens, Chatsworth coming in for a large share. He worked largely in freestone, which carves freely and easily, but weathers badly ; the bulk of his productions are consequently either badly mutilated or altogether destroyed. His best-known works are the two figures representing " Madness " and " Melancholy," executed for the entrance to Bethlehem Hospital, and now in South Kensington Museum.

Grinling Gibbons (1648-1721) was born in Rotterdam, but came to London at the age of 19. Attracting the attention of Evelyn (who records the circum-stance in his " Diary ") he made such an impression upon the Diarist that he introduced Gibbons to a number of prominent artists and architects, including

Sir Peter Lely and Christopher Wren. Gibbons is best known by his wood-carving, in which branch of art he displayed the most marvellous skill, but in addition to wood he worked in stone and bronze. The statue of James II. in the Mall (Plate XLIV.) is a fine example of his work in the latter medium. Besides his work in St. Paul's, in the Chapel of Trinity College, Oxford, on the Archbishop's Throne in Canterbury Cathedral, the altar and pulpit at Fawley Church, Bucks, the pulpit and lectern at St. Bartholomew's, Royal Exchange, and the altar at St. Paul's, Hammersmith, to mention but a few of the churches where he worked, there is also a vast quantity of his work in large country seats throughout England.

Francis Bird (1667-1731) is worthy of notice. Prior to setting up for him-self he found employment with both Grinling Gibbons and Caius Cibber. His best work is perhaps the monument to Dr. Busby, the famous master of West-minster School, in the Abbey. The group in the pediment at the west end of St. Paul's representing the " Conversion of St. Paul," the bas-reliefs under the portico, and five figures of Apostles on the roofs of the transept are his also.

John Michael Rysbrack (1693-1770) executed a number of tombs and other important works for James Gibbs, the architect, after which he started for himself. Amongst his more important individual productions are the tomb of the Duke and Duchess of Marlborough at Blenheim ; the equestrian statue of William III. at Bristol ; the monument to Charles, Duke of Somerset, and his wife in Salisbury Cathedral ; statues of " Hercules " and " Flora," and one of Locke in the Christ Church Library, Oxford. He also executed a number of portrait busts.

Scheemakers (1691-1772) became popular by means of his statue of Shake-speare in Westminster (Plate XLIV.). This monument was designed by Kent and certainly owed some of its popularity to this fact. There are a number of tombs besides this in Westminster for which he was responsible—to Sir John Balchen, to Lord Aubrey Beauclerk, to General Kirk, to Lord Howe, and others.

Louis François Roubiliac (1695-1762) is the best known of the sculptors of this period. His monument to Lady Elizabeth Nightingale in Westminster is certainly an unusual conception. The skeleton with poised dart, and the husband's expression as, in flowing robes, he raises his hand to ward off the fatal thrust aimed by the skeleton at his wife, is a trifle harrowing. But some of the modelling is of a very high standard and there is a good deal of allegorical thought wrapped up in it ; which also applies to the monument to Sir Peter Warren. Other monuments of his are : to the Duke and Duchess of Montagu at Boughton, to Lord Shannon in Walton Church, and to the Lynn family in Southwark Church. His most successful work was not so much in this direction as in his single statues, as Duncan Forbes in Edinburgh, George I. at Cambridge, Sir Isaac Newton at Cambridge, and Shakespeare. A number of busts also stand to his credit—Newton, Ray, and Willoughby, at Trinity College, Cam-bridge ; Spenser, Shakespeare, Milton, Dryden, Pope, Sir Robert Walpole, and others. A number of terra-cotta models and casts of his work are in the British Museum.

We now come to the period which saw the foundation of the Royal Academy. *Joseph Wilton* (1722-1803) was one of the founders of that institution. He studied in Paris and Rome, where he acquired a considerable knowledge of antique sculpture and of anatomy, evidence of which knowledge may be ob-

PLATE XLII.

TOMB OF HENRY VII. IN WESTMINSTER ABBEY. By Torrigiano (16th Century).

PLATE XLIII.

MODELLED ORNAMENT FROM THE NEW RIVER OFFICE, CLERKENWELL.

DETAIL OF MODELLED PLASTER CEILING, WESTWOOD PARK, WORCESTERSHIRE.

served in his work. The monument to General Wolfe in Westminster is one of his most important works. Another of his monuments is that to Admiral Holmes, who is represented in the garb of a Roman citizen, resting his hand on a cannon. This work is well executed, and perhaps the period is to blame for this method of representing a man in a garb he never wore, or dreamed of wearing.

Thomas Banks (1735-1805) worked for some time as a wood-carver, but, as nothing remains, we cannot estimate his ability in this medium. He became a student at the Royal Academy in 1769, being one of the first to attend this institution. After a period of hard work and much disappointment he was elected an A.R.A. in 1784 and a full Member in the following year. Banks was a sculptor who, whilst imbued with a deep love of the classic, yet infused into his work a poetic fervour so often lacking in the work of his contemporaries, who copied the antique forms superficially, and left them cold and lifeless.

Joseph Nollekens (1737-1823) was a pupil of Scheemakers, with whom he served for ten years. At the end of this period he went to Rome, where he met Garrick and Sterne, from both of whom he received a commission for a portrait bust. After ten years in Italy he returned to England and immediately began to receive commissions, particularly for busts. He was made an A.R.A. in 1771 and an R.A. in 1772. He was a hard worker and exhibited a large number of groups, figures, and busts. It is chiefly by his portrait busts that he is remembered. Oliver Goldsmith, Dr. Johnson, William Pitt, Laurence Sterne, Charles James Fox, Spencer Percival, Wellington, Thomas Coutts, Sir Eyre Coote, Lord Erskine, the Hon. Mr. Pelham, and King George III. are but a fraction of the number of eminent men whose features he has perpetuated.

John Bacon (1740-1799) was first apprenticed to Crispe, the maker of the porcelain known as "Bow." He became a student at the Royal Academy, where he worked with Banks and Nollekens among others. He was the first recipient of the Academy Gold Medal for Sculpture, was elected an A.R.A. in 1770 and in 1778 an R.A. His principal work was monumental, and is generally conceived in the broad, simple style best suited to this type of art. The monument to Chatham in the Abbey is a typical example, introducing figures symbolical of Prudence and Fortitude, which though somewhat suave and flamboyant are by no means lacking in good points. His statues of Dr. Johnson and John Howard are much finer examples of his art. Further examples are the memorials to Lord Heathfield, to Lady Millar, to Sir George Pocock, to Samuel Whitbread, to Gray, and to Mason, in Westminster; to the Earl of Tracton (Ireland), to Lord Rodney, to the Earl and Countess of Effingham, to Dr. Anderson (Jamaica), and to Lord Cornwallis (Calcutta). Bacon was more essentially English than his contemporaries. He did not study abroad, and owed little to the antique; but his work has a breadth of style, and a freedom from obtrusive detail quite uncommon amongst the sculptors of his day.

John Flaxman (1755-1826) commenced as a student at the Royal Academy, where Stothard and Blake were his contemporaries. He won the Silver Medal, but failed to obtain the Gold. He was employed by Wedgwood to supply designs for pottery, and much beautiful work exists for which Flaxman was responsible. In 1787 he set out for Rome and the effect of this visit upon one so essentially classic can easily be imagined. He stayed in Rome seven years, and there undertook the series of illustrations to Homer's "Iliad" and "Odyssey" and to Dante's "Divine Comedy" which went far towards establishing his reputation. These drawings are obviously the work of a sculptor, and by their method of treatment suggest low reliefs. Finely composed in the majority of cases, they are excellent examples of economy of line. How deep and earnest was his study of the works in Rome may be gathered from his " Lectures on Sculpture." Returning to England he immediately occupied himself with the tomb of Lord Mansfield (now in the Abbey) which when completed was excellent enough to bring him many commissions, and at the same time influenced the Academicians in their decision to elect him an Associate. This was in 1797 and three years later he became a full Member. In 1810 he was elected to fill the chair of Professor of Sculpture at the Academy, which chair he was the first to occupy. He was indefatigable in his labours, and many examples of his work may be seen in various parts of the Kingdom, the majority of which well repay study. Worthy of mention are : the Baring monument in Micheldever Church ; the memorials to Miss Mary Lushington at Lewisham ; to the Countess Spencer ; to Mrs. Tighe ; to Edward Bulme ; to the Rev. Mr. Clowes in St. John's, Manchester ; to Dr. Warton in Winchester Cathedral ; to Sir Percy Jennings in Lyndhurst Church ; and to Lady Fitzharris in Christchurch Priory. The statues of Warren Hastings, Lord Cornwallis, Coote, Wellesley, and others, executed for the East India House, are also noteworthy. His statue of Sir Joshua Reynolds in St. Paul's (where other examples of his work may be seen) is dignified and well conceived. The shield of Achilles, designed and modelled for Rundell and Bridge (almost his last work) and his statues of Michelangelo and Raphael, may fittingly conclude the list of works by this accomplished sculptor. Flaxman probably had a greater influence upon the art of his day, and he certainly established a wider European reputation, than any other English sculptor up to that time.

Francis Chantrey (1781-1841), after being apprenticed to the grocery business, was articled to Ramsay, a Sheffield carver. In this more congenial atmosphere he worked assiduously, but later severed his connection with Ramsay and set up as a portrait painter. Having accumulated a little money he set out for London, where he worked as a wood-carver, at the same time painting portraits, but always with the ultimate ambition of becoming a sculptor. As a pupil at the Royal Academy he worked diligently at modelling and drawing, but despite his efforts, success was slow in coming to him until he modelled the bust of Horne Tooke, when, so successful was the portrait, commissions rained upon him. In 1816 he was made an A.R.A. and in 1818 a full Member. The " Sleeping Children " in Lichfield Cathedral, was produced about this time, and did much to increase his popularity. There is no space for anything like a complete list of his works ; we must, therefore, content ourselves with a few of his more important ones. A seated figure of Dr. Anderson for Madras ; busts of Canning, Wordsworth, Scott, the Duke of Wellington, George IV., Southey, John Murray, Queen Victoria, Sir Robert Peel, Benjamin West and many others ; monuments to David Pike Watts, the Earl of Malmesbury (in Salisbury Cathedral), to Dr. Digby (in Worcester Cathedral), to Northcote (Exeter), to Mr. and Mrs. Harrison (Sheffield), to Sir Richard Arkwright (Cromford Church), Bishop Heber (St. Paul's), etc., etc. ; statues of Sir Joseph Banks, Canning, Dr. Dalton, Sir John Malcolm (Westminster Abbey), a bronze of Sir William Pitt and others, are but a few of his numerous productions.

English sculpture did not end with Chantrey. In fact it has become revitalised. The pseudo-classical influence has been cast off almost entirely,

PLATE XLIV.

(c) PART OF A MEMORIAL TO THE DUKE OF WELLINGTON.
By Alfred Stevens.

(b) SHAKESPEARE MEMORIAL IN WESTMINSTER ABBEY.
By Scheemakers.

(a) STATUE OF JAMES II.
By Grinling Gibbons.

PLATE XLV.

(a) "PHYSICAL ENERGY." By G. F. Watts, R.A.

(b) "DANAÏDES." By Auguste Rodin.

and the men of to-day, while admitting their indebtedness to the great ones of the past, are working more independently than did those of the Early Victorian era. It is impossible here to deal with each man individually or to give any-thing like a complete account of the work executed. A few names and examples must suffice, and more particularly those who belong to the last generation.

Alfred Stevens, whose work was obviously inspired by that of the Italian Renaissance, cannot be ignored. His Wellington monument in St. Paul's is one of the finest architectural and sculptural conceptions of late years. Plate XLIV. is a portion of this great work.

G. F. Watts, whose equestrian statue " Physical Energy," or " Progress " as it is sometimes called (Plate XLV.), and " Clytie " bear distinct traces of Greek influence, is also worthy of mention. His work is an unusual blend of classic form, inspired by Celtic mysticism. " Progress " is a youthful figure, mounted on a horse that vibrates with energy and eagerness to be away, while the rider peers with thoughtful gaze far into the future. This statue was modelled with plaster mixed with tow applied to an armature of iron. It is of colossal size, and this method of working possesses distinct advantages for statues of large size. " Clytie," though Hellenic in treatment and conception, has more movement, more of the fervid energy that characterises modern thought, than of the calm serenity that marked the work of Greece.

Lord Leighton was also inspired by Hellenic art. His forms are classic, though his " Athlete Struggling with Python " is fraught with the restlessness, the ceaseless striving that differentiates this era from the Hellenic. The " Sluggard," too, suggests a tired youth, or one who has just awakened from sleep, endeavouring to shake off sloth by an energetic stretching of his muscles. Hellenic in form, but conceived in the spirit of the age. Leighton was too true an artist to work in an outworn style, or to express ideas that the world had outgrown.

Alfred Gilbert must be mentioned, for he has produced some exquisite work, largely influenced by the Italian Renaissance. There is no space here to deal with the more modern men, as *Hamo Thorneycroft, Sir Thomas Brock, Sir George Frampton, Colton, Harry Bates, Swan, Goscombe John, Gilbert Bayes, Onslow Ford* and many others, and it would be invidious to select a few when so many are good. But the general trend of modern sculpture seems to be a decorative one. The best work is marked by a fine restraint and a keen sense of line and mass that suggests a sound and scholarly knowledge of technique, and if a national school of sculpture is to grow up it is undoubtedly along these lines that it will develop.

INDEX.

ABERDEEN : THE UNIVERSITY PRESS.